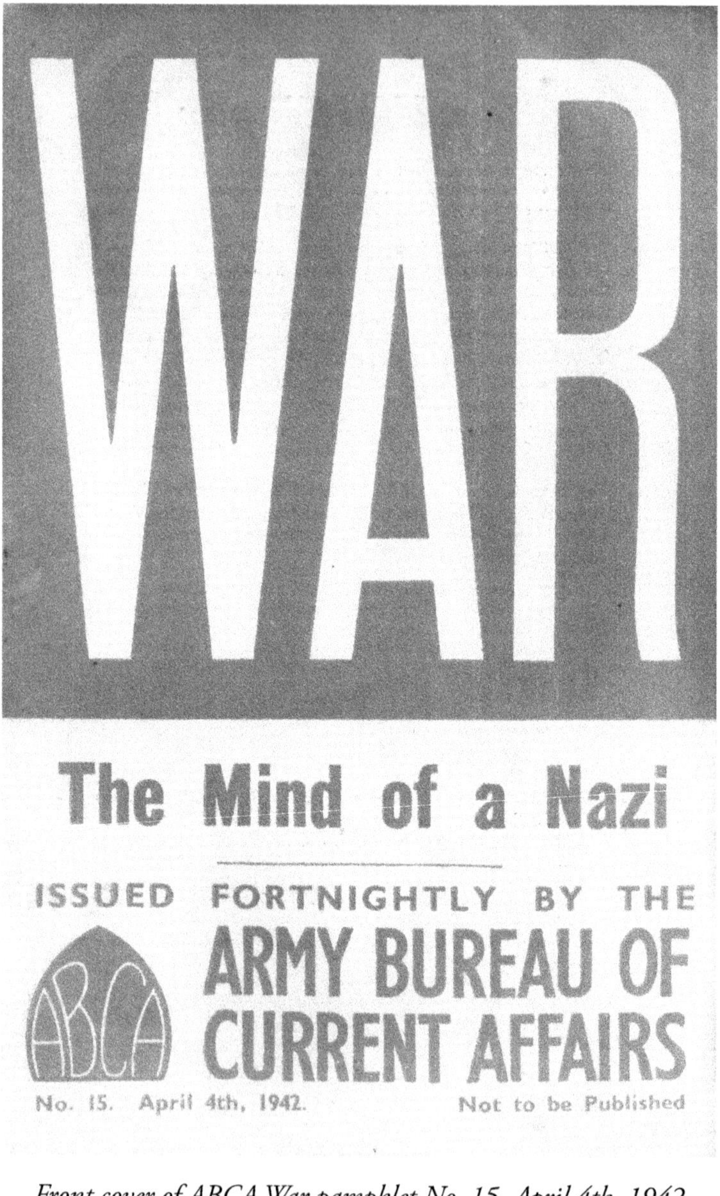
WAR
The Mind of a Nazi
ISSUED FORTNIGHTLY BY THE
ARMY BUREAU OF
CURRENT AFFAIRS
ABCA
No. 15. April 4th, 1942.
Not to be Published

Front cover of ABCA War pamphlet No. 15, April 4th, 1942

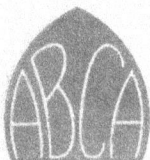

NAZIS

British Views on Germany during the Second World War

Army Bureau of Current Affairs

First published by the Army Bureau of Current Affairs 1942-43.
This compilation published by Books Ulster in 2016.

Typographical arrangement © Books Ulster

ISBN: 978-1-910375-45-7

All rights reserved. No part of this publication may be reproduced, stored in a retrieval system, or transmitted by any means, electronic, mechanical, photocopying or otherwise, without the prior permission of the publisher.

Foreword

In *Nazis: British Views on Germany during the Second World War* is to be found not only an excellent overview of the development of Nazism and the causes of the war, but also a genuinely revealing insight into the mindset of the German soldier and people. The book comprises a selection of articles from 1942-3 that originally appeared in the *War* and *Current Affairs* series of pamphlets published by the Army Bureau of Current Affairs for the education of British servicemen. Among the contributions is an eye-witness account of the Germans marching into Paris that provides some interesting details on the nature of the early occupation of the city. Much of the information on the Nazi mentality contained within the articles was gleaned from Germans taken prisoner in Europe, the Middle East and Africa.

The ABCA, widely regarded as being left-wing in nature, puts across a message in these pieces that is both striking and quite unequivocal—the Nazis are out for world domination and the effective enslavement of the rest of Europe to serve the Reich's needs; war against Germany is not only justified, but absolutely necessary in order to save civilisation from regression and descent into barbarism:

> 'This is a war in which the whole future of our civilisation will be decided. It is a war whose outcome will affect every single one of us. We are fighting against a system which is based on brutal force, on the wicked and unchristian claim that there is one master race whose self-appointed leader can determine the fate of millions of civilised and freedom-loving human beings, a system by which the Nazi leaders seek to set up a rule of oppression and exploitation such as the world has never seen before and by which they want to put the clock back by at least five hundred years.'

The advocacy for post-war European unity is also clearly stated:

> 'Although Europe is the second smallest continent, it is perhaps the most important one of all. It is the cradle of Western civilisation and events that have taken place in it have influenced the fate of almost the whole world. On the other hand Europe is politically more disunited than any of the other continents. It is split up into a number of independent states which have waged war among themselves almost without a break. Several of these wars have engulfed large parts of the entire world. It is not surprising, therefore, that people should have dreamed of a united Europe which would use its vast resources in the interests of all the European nations. Even if such far-reaching ideals as that of a United States of Europe were rejected as utopian and unpractical, many people thought that there should at least be economic unity.'

The contents of this book were not written with the benefit of hindsight and yet a quiet confidence that Nazism would ultimately be defeated pervades the text. As general context to the Second World War, and for a sense of the times, this collection of writing is a truly invaluable resource.

A number of footnotes have been added in this edition for the benefit of those who may be unfamiliar with some of the events and people referred to in the text.

Derek Rowlinson

Contents

The Mind of a Nazi	1
The German Army	11
Hitler's Own War	25
What a Nazi Soldier Thinks	53
The Development of Nazism	59
The first time they saw Paris	85
Germany's New Order	91
The Trouble With Germans	117

WAR

The Mind of a Nazi

ABCA 'War' Pamphlet No. 15, April 4th, 1942

To all Officers

Information given in WAR is not to be communicated either directly or indirectly to the Press, or to any person not holding an official position in His Majesty's Forces.

WAR is one of the two fortnightly bulletins of ABCA—the Army Bureau of Current Affairs, created by the Army Council to "brief" officers for talks to their men on war topics and to provide them with informative "background" on varied aspects of the war. Contributions and correspondence for WAR should be addressed to the Army Bureau of Current Affairs, Curzon Street House, Curzon Street, London, W.I.—and envelopes marked WAR Contributions may be submitted direct on being initialled by the writer's Commanding Officer. Contributions for Quiz are also invited.

- *The German fighting man—as seen by an Interrogation Officer who has dealt with many prisoners during the war.*

The Mind of a Nazi

A PARTY of half a dozen German prisoners of war was being driven from one London terminus to another on their way to prison camp. They were N.C.O.s of the Luftwaffe, survivors of the crews of German raiders shot down over this country.

They looked around them with the greatest interest as they drove along, taking in every detail of the traffic, the pedestrians and the buildings they passed. Now and again, as they went by a shop or a house damaged in air raids, they would nudge one another furtively and jerk their heads in its direction.

The British officer in charge of the escort called out cheerfully in German to one of them, a 21-year-old radio operator from a bomber: "You see, there are still a few buildings standing here!" The man smiled knowingly: "Ah, but you are making big detours all the time so that we shall not see the real damage," he answered.

A little later, when the car was held up by traffic lights outside a well-stocked provision shop, the officer tried again: "Well, anyway, you see we still have something to eat!" The prisoner was not impressed. "Yes, just for show, in the shops we are passing," he replied.

You can't fool me!

The man was not being insolent. He was speaking what he honestly thought to be the truth, and he, no doubt, expected to make an impression by his smartness in seeing through "British propaganda tricks." For the last nine years, in Nazi Germany, he had been brought up to believe, not the evidence of his senses, but what German propaganda told him. The German wireless and newspapers had told him that London was flat and the shops empty. For him, therefore, London *was* flat and the shops *were* empty.

But what was he to think when he actually found himself in London and saw that, to all appearances, life was going on more or less as usual there? Was he to believe his own eyes or German propaganda? He did not hesitate. He believed German propaganda.

The only explanation he could think of for what he saw was that we had taken the trouble to cart half a dozen German N.C.O. prisoners all over London so as to avoid their seeing the places where the bombs had fallen, and that, furthermore, we displayed our last few provisions in special shops along their route just to impress them.

Everyone who has come into contact with German prisoners would be able to cite similar instances. There is the case of the German airman who landed by parachute during the Battle of Britain. Before he set out on what was to be his last flight he had been told that the invasion and conquest of Britain were imminent. He therefore hid in some woods close to where he landed for a couple of days, and then boldly emerged and ordered the first person he met to take him to the occupied zone of Britain. He was so sure that during the couple of days he had been in hiding the Germans must have landed and already occupied large areas.

V for Viktoria

Another instance concerns the "V for Victory" campaign. When the German propaganda authorities found they could not stop it spreading in the occupied territories on the Continent, they took it over themselves, pretending it was their own idea. It was a pitiful crib, because not one German in ten had ever heard of the word "Viktoria" which, Goebbels assured them, meant "victory." The usual German word for "victory" is "Sieg."

A German petty-officer, prisoner from a U-boat, on landing at a Scottish port was greeted by street-urchins making the "V" sign to him with their fingers. During conversation with an interrogation officer later on it turned out that the U-boat man was convinced that the Scottish children had been won over by Dr. Goebbels' "V für Viktoria" campaign and that they were waiting to welcome the victorious German troops when they came to conquer Britain.

Leave it to the Others

These are just a few of the many examples which could be given to show how completely the great majority of German prisoners of war are under the influence of Nazi propaganda—and prisoners of war are, of course, just random specimens from the various German fighting services.

After a few weeks most of them have to admit that conditions in England are far better than they had been led to believe. Some of them, on thinking things over, realise that their own branch of the German fighting forces is not as invincible as they had imagined. But they are still sure that Germany must win the war, so they count on other services doing the job. U-boat prisoners who have seen for themselves how British convoys are getting through, and that the U-boats are having a thin time, say: "The U-boat weapon is out of date. Your modern counter-measures are too good. But our army and air force will do the trick."

In the same way captured airmen think things over and comfort themselves with the assurance that the U-boats and the army will be successful, the infantryman decides he can leave things to the Panzers, and so on. The Italians decide that Italy cannot do much, anyhow, and pin their faith on the Germans.*

The Making of a Nazi

The question naturally arises—how on earth was the ordinary, average German brought into this frame of mind? Take the case

---

* In *The Trouble with Italians*, ABCA *War* pamphlet No. 35, January 9th, 1943, Lieut. Richard Bennett gives a 'summary and estimate' of the Italian army and discusses the Italian soldier's apparent lack of appetite for the fight.

of the Luftwaffe N.C.O. mentioned earlier. He was a 12-year-old schoolboy when Hitler came to power, and was just beginning to read his first elementary history book. The books previously in use had been withdrawn by the Nazis and scrapped, and in their place new books had been issued, specially written by the German Propaganda Ministry.

They were still called history books, and the 12-year-old schoolboy thought it was history he was reading in them. They told him, above all, that Germany was not really beaten in the last war. That she was, in fact, on the point of winning, when the simple, kind-hearted German people were tricked into peace by the Allies and "betrayed" by German Socialists in foreign pay.

Books on other subjects were similarly full of lies. Teachers were forced to drill the children into becoming good little Nazis. In their spare time the children, instead of playing and doing homework, were given more drill. Our Luftwaffe N.C.O., at the age of 12, joined the Hitler Young Folk organisation, and learnt to obey orders. At the age of 14 he joined the Hitler Youth, where drilling and discipline were stricter. He had already reached the stage when his parents would not have dared to tell him that what he was being taught was nonsense, for fear he might repeat it and get them into trouble.

Ready for Rotterdam

At the age of 17, having completed his apprenticeship at some trade or other, he was conscripted for his six months in the Labour Service, where he slogged in a gang all day and listened to Nazi speeches, lectures and march tunes in the evening. And all the time, whenever he picked up a newspaper, switched on the wireless, went to the pictures or a theatre, the idea was dinned into him—sometimes directly, sometimes more subtly: "Never think for yourself. Just obey orders. Leave it all to Hitler. Hitler is a super-man who cannot make a mistake. Don't bother about conscience or religion. What Hitler tells you to do is right."

The Mind of a Nazi

In this way Hitler finally got the German people into the mental state he needed. Our Luftwaffe N.C.O. and the other young men, and many, but not all, of the older men, were ready and eager to go to war, to go anywhere Hitler cared to send them, carrying death, destruction and misery to any neighbour that happened to be smaller, weaker, less well-armed, less ruthless and brutal than themselves.

Ready to bomb defenceless Rotterdam to ruins, killing 30,000 civilians in a few hours,* ready to cruise over Belgrade, dropping ton after ton of bombs until the city was just wiped out, ready to machine-gun roads choked with terrified French and Belgian refugees, as part of a deliberate military plan.

Men who have done these things without a qualm have later on been taken prisoner in other and sterner combats in which the odds have not been quite so overwhelmingly on their side. Many of them are obviously proud of what they have done, few of them see the enormity of it.

Those "Inferior People"

When asked for their opinion of the Rotterdam massacre, most German prisoners will say quite seriously: "That was nothing to do with us—that was the fault of the Dutch for not surrendering when we told them to." All conception of justice and fairness has, in the course of eight years, been deliberately ground out of them in accordance with a well-laid plan for making men brutes. The following dialogue, which took place between a British interrogation officer and a German prisoner, is typical:—

Officer: "Aren't you surprised at being treated so decently as a prisoner after the way you have behaved to beaten enemies?"

---

* The 'Rotterdam Blitz' took place under controversial circumstances on May 14th, 1940. Subsequent estimates put the casualties at under 1,000, but the number made homeless at over 80,000.

Prisoner: "We always treat our prisoners well."
Officer: "How about the Poles, the Czechs and the Jews?"
Prisoner: "Oh, them! They are inferior people."

They Are No Weaklings

The great majority of German officers, although, of course, better educated in technical subjects, have more or less the same Nazi mass-mentality. There are, of course, some exceptions among both officers and men, especially those of the older classes. Many of the older men look on the Nazi youngsters as bumptious, ignorant louts.

We must, of course, be careful not to under-rate the enemy. It has, for example, often been asserted that the physique of German youth has suffered as a result of privations during and just after the last war. Hitler, of course, has squealed louder on this subject than anybody else. Let it be stated with all emphasis that those who have come into contact with German prisoners have seen but few signs of physical weakness. It is possible that the weaklings have not yet been called up, or that they have not yet gone into action. In any case the prisoners so far dealt with have been of good health and sound physique.

Furthermore, they have been well looked after and well fed, both during training and on active service. The German frontline soldiers of all services eat like lords compared with the rest of the population.

Praise for Their Officers

Another point which has emerged from interrogation of prisoners concerns the relations between officers and men. Hitler has seen the disadvantages of the impassable barrier with which the old Prussian military caste surrounded itself in its relations with the ranks, and has gone to great pains to introduce a spirit of friendliness. In this he seems to have had considerable success.

With the inevitable exceptions, captured prisoners speak in high terms of their officers. They frequently tell of friendly, informal relations when off-duty, and how these are achieved without any laxity in respect of discipline.

We all know that Hitler has given just as much attention to the military training and equipment of his soldiers as he has to the conditioning of their minds. In most cases, interrogation shows that the prisoner's training has been long and good. But it is also clear to those who have been in contact with German prisoners that Hitler, for all his efforts, has not produced the perfect soldier. The Nazi system, for all its Teutonic thoroughness, has some vital faults.

Can't Have It Both Ways

Firstly, it is impossible to teach a man to stop using his intelligence and imagination with regard to life in general without impairing these faculties in their application to one particular subject—namely, warfare. Either a man is generally alert, quick, enquiring, imaginative —or he is not. These are not qualities which can be turned on, like a tap, for one subject and turned off for all the rest.

The Nazis may have sensed this weakness, for they have tried, by a most thorough training—this applies mainly to armoured and other special troops—to teach their soldiers, N.C.O.s and officers the answer to any conceivable situation which may arise on the battlefield. They have much experience in modern warfare, and can foresee many emergencies—but sooner or later in a fast-moving battle an emergency will crop up which has not been foreseen, and then the soldier with the freer, quicker, more responsive mind will use his initiative and come off best.

The Answer In Russia?

The second weakness may be expected to reveal itself in the

morale of the German troops, especially of the masses of infantry in a long and gruelling campaign. When these men, brought up in the belief of their own invincibility and their Fuehrer's infallibility, have it gradually dinned into them by repeated hard knocks that these beliefs are illusions, that the Fuehrer has committed some awful howlers and they are the dupes of the biggest political swindle in history, what will their reactions be?

It may be that we are beginning to see the answer to this question in Russia, where the impetus and enthusiasm of the victorious German onrush has been worn down to deadlock and retreat by the unflinching determination of the Soviet armies.* It is also significant that Rommel, in Libya, before he launched his picked Panzer troops into action, thought it necessary to stimulate them with false reports that Moscow had been captured.

---

* Articles on Russia and the Red Army's fight against the Nazis can be found in ABCA's *War* series, nos. 18, 38 & 90, and *Current Affairs*, nos. 25, 57 & 103A, inter alia.

WAR

The German Army

ABCA 'War' Pamphlet No. 17, May 2nd, 1942

Know Him?

He is a lance-corporal of the German infantry in field service uniform. His steel helmet is the standard model for all ranks. He often wears under it his greenish-grey cloth forage cap. His tunic is also grey-green, with a darker collar which may be folded back and left open at the neck. His trousers are grey, tucked into half-jack boots. His belt is of soft, black leather with a dull white-metal buckle and cartridge pouches attached. His equipment includes a pack, bivouac sheet with cords, water-bottle, respirator (which he is not wearing in the drawing), gas cape, entrenching tool, and sidearms.

The arm of his service can be seen from the colour of the piping on his shoulder strap, in this case white for infantry. In the field all other identifications, such as the figure "3" for his company and "6" for his regiment would have been removed. The collar patch also indicates by colour his arm of the service. The arm badge shows his rank.

[The above image is taken from the inside cover of WAR pamphlet No. 16, April 18th, 1942]

How Would You Know It?

The answer is because no British armoured car has eight wheels. This is the standard heavy German armoured car of which there are large numbers. It is 17ft. long and 9ft. high, weighs 9-10 tons, and carries a crew of four or five. It has 30mm. armour plate, one 2 cm. (.79in.) gun and one L.M.G. It has a 90-100 h.p. rear engine, a maximum road speed of 53 m.p.h., and is noted for quiet running.

[The above image is taken from the inside cover of WAR pamphlet No. 17, May 2nd, 1942]

How Would You Know It?

It looks old-fashioned. Its shield is in two sections, with a vision slit in the left one. It has large wheels with steel rims or solid rubber tyres. Usually to be found sited well forward and sometimes mistaken for divisional artillery. Actually it is the 15 cm. (5.91 ins.) heavy infantry gun of the German infantry regiment, each regiment (equivalent of our brigade) having two of these, as well as six light guns, for close support. Range: approximately 6,000 yards, with an 80-lb. shell, firing four rounds a minute.

[The above image is taken from the inside cover of WAR pamphlet No. 18, May 16th, 1942]

The Man We're Up Against

The German Army

This is the first of a series of articles which will appear in WAR from time to time under the general title, "The Man We' re Up Against." Here is presented an authentic picture of the German Army, its background and the men who serve in it—written by a British senior officer who had personal contact with the German Army in the years immediately preceding the war.

FREDERICK THE GREAT inherited from his father Frederick William, known as the "soldier King," a standing army fourth in numbers and probably first in training and discipline of the continental armies of the day—a force famous for the exactness of its drill at a time when steadiness of drill in the mass was the first tactical requisite on the battle-field; and the earliest army ever trained to march in step. This force, used by Frederick in unscrupulous and desperate adventures, which exhausted but also inspired his country, laid the foundations of modern Prussia.

When at Frederick's death the directing genius failed, the whole organism decayed; and the Prussian power was soon afterwards completely overwhelmed by the revolutionary armies of Napoleon. The six years of subjection to France which followed produced a truly national reaction. It was a citizen army which, hurriedly improvised in 1813, helped to bring Napoleon down; and the reformers, who now for the first time introduced universal military service, valued this militia spirit highly, and did all they could to encourage it.

But that spirit, associated with the liberalism of the time, perished in the political conflicts of the first part of the nineteenth century. By the 'fifties the army was once more a professional preserve, officered almost entirely by the aristocracy and tending to stagnation; conscientious, but thoroughly dull. No one would have expected that it was soon to upset the whole balance of Europe.

They Learned Lessons

The Franco-Austrian War of 1859 gave the Prussian Government the opportunity of discovering, without themselves being put to the test, the shortcomings of their forces. The occasion was not missed, and produced the men to grasp it—Bismarck, the statesman, who forced through his army reforms in the face of Parliament, and Moltke, the creator of the Great General Staff. Between them they created the army which in 1866, in a campaign of six weeks, set Prussia once for all in Austria's place as the chief German power; and which in 1870-1 destroyed the French Second Empire and reduced France to a decided military inferiority.

They had good material to work on. The high standard of education in Prussia earned for the battle of Königgrätz, which decided the Austrian war, the name of the "schoolmaster's victory." The army, greatly enlarged by Bismarck, was armed with the new "needle-gun" or breech-loading rifle, which increased greatly the fire power of the infantry; and the General Staff under Moltke was the first to realise the immense changes in strategic tempo made possible, since the Napoleonic Wars, by the introduction of railways and telegraphs.

The Soldier's Prestige

Bismarck, by not going too far, was able to hold what he had won. No sudden downfall or revenge of fate undid his victories. The spirit of Prussian militarism, feeding on its own success, grew almost unchallenged; and all the while Germany was undergoing the far-reaching and rapid industrialisation which was to enable her to sustain war so well upon the modern scale.

Nothing could be stronger proof of the military instincts of the

German people than their ability, through a whole generation of unbroken peace, to maintain the condition of their army. Twenty or thirty years of rest after victory have often proved enough for a tested military system to fall into disrepair. But the German Army was never readier for war, nor its efficiency higher, than in 1914. The General Staff did its work with thorough care; and the military enjoyed an unequalled social prestige.

The story of the Hauptmann von Köpenick belongs most truly to this period. This little saddler for a hoax disguised himself as a Prussian officer, fell in a squad of soldiers, marched them to the station, commandeered transport to a neighbouring town and arrested the Mayor, all without anyone's daring to stop him. This story is not a satire, it is true.

Deadlock in the Trenches

The Great War of 1914-18 produced a sequence of brilliant German professional successes on the Eastern front. Serbia, Rumania and Russia were overrun or shattered. But in the west, after the initial blow had failed, the military science of both sides came to a deadlock in the trenches, which only the combined pressure of land and sea power was able to resolve. When it seemed that the Allied offensives could make no head against Germany on land, that pressure drove Ludendorff in turn to stake everything on a great offensive of his own; and when this failed, and then recoiled, he was beaten. The Allied counter-attacks drove him back with increasing speed from the Marne and Amiens to the Belgian frontier. The Balkan front collapsed, and his fate was decided. At the end of September, 1918, Ludendorff himself gave orders to seek an Armistice. The German Army had been decisively beaten in the field.

The Treaty of Versailles abolished conscription in Germany, and allowed the new republic a long service army of only 100,000 men, without tanks, aircraft or heavy artillery. The stages by which these limits were first evaded and then repudiated are well known.

The 100,000 Army

In March, 1935, Hitler re-introduced universal military service, and next year raised the army to 36 divisions, and at the same time the great rearmament began. He had at his disposal an obedient people, a well-equipped though rather rusty industry, and four or five years; and he made full use of them all. The members of the "100,000 Army" became officers and N.C.Os. in Hitler's new army. He had, too, a clear field for the standardisation of military equipment which is characteristic of his armies to-day. He commenced forming the Panzer divisions which were to prove so formidable later.

The great German General Staff was revived in all its ancient glory. A combined staff containing representatives of all three services was set up in Berlin. The task of this staff, under its chief, was to dictate the nation's military policy, both strategic and economic, for all these services. It contained a "War Economics" section, which assisted at its labours. While this central staff dictated policy, the Ministries of War, Navy and Air were responsible for all the executive work resulting from that policy. No one service was predominant, although it was tacitly admitted that for Germany, a continental nation, the army was the most important thing, and that it would be the army which in the end would win a war for Germany.

Mobilisation System

For the purpose of recruiting and military administration, Germany, now including Austria, the Protectorate, Danzig and Posen, is divided into 18 military administrative areas, and these again into a hierarchy of small units. In peace-time each area furnished one corps. On mobilisation these corps took the field under their area commanders, and the area remained under the administrative command of a deputy G.O.C., the depots being occupied by depot units of the "Ersatzheer," or Reserve Army. Such, at least, is the basis of the system; though its regularity has now been modified by the grouping of certain reserve units into reserve divisions serving as low category formations in the Field Army. It is to these units that the recruit is first drafted.

But the working of conscription in Nazi Germany cannot be understood without a view of the pre-military training to which German youth has been subjected. From the age of 12, German boys have, since 1933, been drilled in youth organisations only nominally voluntary, and all directed to the upbringing of Nazi soldiers. Two things have been taught them—first, a soldierly ability to live hard: second, an unquestioning respect for authority. This combination provides the army with material that is, within its limitations, formidable.

Besides membership of these organisations every youth has also, or had, after enlistment but before his military service, to undergo six months' labour service on land reclamation and other similar undertakings. This labour service, though now sometimes omitted, has been a most important Nazi institution. Every advantage has been taken of the opportunities which the system afforded for relentless Nazification. Each evening has been spent in the organised absorbing of propaganda. Drill, harangues and community singing have filled every minute of spare time. And yet the most sinister thing perhaps is not that German youth should be subjected to this process, but that they should enjoy it.

It follows that when the peace-time conscript finally arrived at his two years' military service, it appeared more like a promotion than an interruption of his career. Life was more interesting and probably more comfortable than what he had recently known. The lessons of discipline had already been learnt; and he passed at once to the acquiring of that professional competence which marks the German soldier.

Hitler's Knowledge

Hitler's absorbing interest has been his Army, much more than his Air Force or Navy. He has himself considerable detailed military knowledge and much of the Siegfried Line, Germany's defence against France, was personally designed by him. He has, by constant visits and inspections, encouraged officers and men and assured himself of their general efficiency. The army is loyal to Hitler and admires him.

The German soldier of to-day is taught obedience, but not blind obedience. Discipline is strict, the Germans believing that "spit and polish" is an essential in all military training. A German soldier may look dirty and untidy while on manoeuvres or training, but on guards or after duty and when walking out he turns out clean and smart and takes a real pride in his appearance. No error or misdemeanour is, however, too unimportant to be checked and the Prussian serjeant-major is no legend. It is fundamental that every error, every mistake, however small or even apparently trivial, should be noticed and corrected. On the other hand relations between officers and men are not only good but often cordial. An officer looks upon his men as his children to some extent. This does not prevent him, however, demanding from them the greatest sacrifices if necessary.

Both men and officers were accommodated before the war in excellent barracks, but the standard of food did not compare favourably with that served in the British Army. There was little time for sport, so much had to be learnt in the two years that they were with the army.

Training is Realistic

German military training was and is hard and realistic. Casualties in the last manoeuvres before the war were reported to be about four hundred. Great attention has always been paid to fitness (they attributed our success in the last war principally to our physical fitness and love of games), and the hours of work, even before the war, were long and arduous. The army was trained for a Blitzkrieg. Speed was the essential in all military operations. "Push on" at any price; to do nothing is to commit a major military crime, was continually drummed into every officer and man. Supporting weapons co-operated closely with the infantry. The Germans maintain that it is the infantry alone which in the end wins battles. The Panzer divisions and the dive bomber exist only to put the infantry on to the objective. German propaganda never fails to point out that infantry is still "Queen of the Battlefield."

German orders differ considerably from ours. There is no hard and fast sequence for them. Generally speaking, the smaller the operation the more detailed the orders. An operation order for the move of a corps may consist of six to seven lines only.

German "Battle Drill"

The German Army is an exponent of "battle drill." For this reason their methods have often been described as "stereotyped."

This is, however, quite a wrong conception of German tactics. The Germans insist that certain things must be carried out in a certain way, e.g., a frontal attack will, when possible, be combined with a flank attack whether the attack is being carried out by a section or an army. Within this framework, however, the German officer, N.C.O. and man is left great latitude.

A task is set with clearly defined limits, but within these limits the maximum initiative is encouraged and demanded. There is, in fact, no bar on initiative provided the fundamentals of "battle drill" are observed. But the initiative shown must be "trained initiative," based on knowledge and not ignorance. "All formalism in tactics is bad" say German military publications. "Success in battle depends on the determination of the individual" is an axiom.

Assault parties, creeping forward with explosives and perhaps flame throwers, are a normal feature of infantry technique: so normal, indeed, that a humorous article in a German paper gives the following advice to troops on leave (if they ever get it—for German troops in war-time get very little). When they return home from Russia to the unfamiliar surroundings of Germany they must be careful to respect civilian habits almost forgotten at the front. If the front door is shut, the proper thing is not to blow it open with a charge in the usual way; for the custom of the country is to ring the bell.

Far From Home

This story throws light on a grievance which German troops often feel. Their pay is good, their rations much better than those of civilians; but leave is very scarce, and they hate being away from home. They have, besides, home anxieties of a kind foreign to us. The files of a Coast Defence Battery in Norway contain a curious instance of the complexities of German life and administration.

Gunner Palenga's home is in Silesia, near a thousand miles away. There his wife lives with her mother. The mother comes under the displeasure of the Party, and is given notice to quit her house. He has to get his battery commander to write to the municipal authorities to plead against an order which would turn a serving soldier's wife into the street. Fortunately, he was in time. The officer's application caused the order to be suspended—but only suspended.

Thorough Preparations

The German General Staff, in fact all German officers, are keen students of military history. They examine and re-examine the lessons of past wars in order to deduce from them the main lessons. They believe that preparations are three-quarters of the battle.

German attack tactics are simple and can be explained in a few sentences. The attackers first of all select a point at which they will make their main effort. This they call a "Schwerpunkt," or point of main effort. The German officer is taught "An attack without a Schwerpunkt is like a man without character," but if he has chosen the wrong point for his Schwerpunkt he is prepared to change it immediately.

If the battle is an encounter battle, e.g., an advanced guard action, they are prepared to run great risks, even to the length of dispensing with reconnaissance in order to surprise and overwhelm the enemy before he has time to take counter-measures. They invariably try to combine a frontal attack with an outflanking attack.

Trained for Offensive

On the other hand, for a deliberate attack no preparation can be too careful. Reconnaissance after reconnaissance is carried out in order that all commanders should have the best information about the enemy. Every man, weapon and machine is then thrown into the battle at the spot where they hope to obtain a decisive result. Again they try to combine a frontal with a flank attack.

Infiltration tactics are an essential part of all attacks, whether frontal or flanking.

In defence there is one cardinal principle—depth. "Not lines but localities must be defended. Fire is the principal weapon of the defence." So runs the German doctrine. The German Army, however, is primarily trained for the offensive. It dislikes assuming the defensive because it knows that it can never obtain a decision by that means. The present defensive battles on the Russian front are regarded as a prelude to offensive operations and not of any military value in themselves.

When the German Army took the field in 1939 it was an army with a tradition of defeat behind it. Its successes in this war have, to some extent, eradicated this feeling, but even now, at the back of the minds of all German officers and men is the knowledge that in 1918 the Germany Army was decisively beaten in the field. Two of its former opponents, the British Empire and the U.S.A., are again ranged against it and the German soldier must feel that these two opponents will in the end get the better of him. His determination will not, however, be easily broken. He is cunning and crafty and an aptitude for soldiering is in his blood. He is also tough, otherwise he would not have stood the strain of this war.

CURRENT AFFAIRS

Hitler's Own War

ABCA 'Current Affairs' Pamphlet No. 21, July 4th, 1942

PUT THIS OVER

THIS bulletin deals with a topic more immediately important to your men than any other subject whatever. One difference between a democratic citizen and a fascist is that the former has the right to hear and discuss the reasons why he is called to arms.

Many of us are perhaps inclined, once we join the Army, to forget or disregard what brought us there. It is possibly true that a man will fight even if he doesn't know what it's all about. But that is a dumb and undignified way of fighting. The best soldier is the one whose skill and valour are fortified by the knowledge that the cause for which he goes into action is a damned sight better than his opponent's.

The reasons why the Allied Nations took arms against Hitler are clearly set out by Harold Nicolson in this bulletin. They are not a matter of opinion, but a matter of cold, conclusive fact. If you can put them over to your men they will recognise the overwhelming force of the Allied case, and they will be reinvigorated by the positive certainty that there can only be one answer to German tyranny and aggression.

A good way to tackle this subject is to "take soundings" by way of a few questions: "Why did we go to war with Germany?" "What territories did Hitler invade since 1936?" "What did we do to prevent war?" These questions will serve a double purpose: (a) to give you an idea of how much or how little your men know of pre-war history; (b) to show you what particular points in this bulletin you need to emphasise in your talk.

Officers who have a high proportion of young soldiers in their unit should treat this topic with exceptional care. Many serving soldiers were in their 'teens when this war began, and therefore—like most youths—weren't at that time bothering their heads about current affairs. These are the men, more than any others, who must be shown the reasons why we are at war. Unless they learn those reasons in the Army they will never understand them properly.

Use this opportunity, above all, to make your men feel something like this when the discussion is over: "Well, there may be a lot wrong with Army life, and I'll never give up my grouses. But the only answer to make to the gang that let us in for this little lot is to go after them and knock them out once and for all." If you put this bulletin across, that is the response you are sure to get.

Why We Are at War With Germany

By HAROLD NICOLSON

The Hon. Harold Nicolson, C.M.G., M.P., is a Governor of the B.B.C and is well known both as a writer and broadcaster. *

1. None Of Us Wanted War

WHEN I meet people in trains (and I find that nowadays I meet many people in trains) I sometimes ask them a question. "Tell me," I say, "why are we at war with Germany?"

I find that eight people out of every ten are totally unable to answer this question and gaze at me with suspicion, imagining that I am a Fifth Columnist seeking to spread despondency or to entice them into careless talk. Very rarely I get the correct answer, couched in the simple phrase: "Well, I suppose it was about time that we told Hitler where he got off." And quite often I find people who give me some stock answer which they have derived from sources other than their own knowledge, thoughts or feelings. "It was all," such people say, "the fault of the bankers and capitalists." Or "It was all the fault of our diplomacy which allowed us to become tied up to foreign countries." It seems strange to me that any serious person can believe that the capitalists could have desired a war which will quite certainly put an end to the delights of capitalism. Nor do I quite understand, if this version

---

* Harold Nicolson (1886-1968) was married to the writer Vita Sackville-West with whom he had a rather unorthodox relationship. His *Diaries and Letters* 1930–1939 and 1939–1945 provide a useful resource on the prologue to war and on the Second World War itself.

be true, how we are to account for the fact that Russia (a country in which there are comparatively few capitalists) should also have been drawn into a war on the side of the rich. And how comes it, if the isolationists are correct in what they say, that the United States (which to our distress has for more than 20 years kept aloof from all European entanglements) should also have become one of the belligerents? The fact is that none of the countries fighting on our side wanted war; war was thrust upon them; so that the question really ought to be: "Why were we unable to avoid this war?" But however we frame the question, we must recognise that it is a question which needs answering. Each one of us in fact should try to be clear in his own mind why we are now at war with Germany. We must get the whole thing into correct focus and not allow the foreground to become confused with the background. For if we have but a hazy or incorrect conception of the *causes* of this war we shall find ourselves becoming equally vague regarding its *purposes*. Conversely, once we have a clear answer to the question: "Why are we fighting?" we shall have gone a long way towards answering that other question: "What are we fighting for?"

I. The German Version

2. The German Excuse

In the long history of human conflict it has been customary for each side to assert that the other side hit him first. The Germans cannot quite say that, since even the most brilliant propaganda will not make people believe, for instance, that that great bully Denmark suddenly rose and struck poor little Germany on the nose. They therefore obscure the issue by raising a vast smoke-screen of "rights" and "sufferings." They say that the Treaty of Versailles was a brutal treaty, that it robbed them of all raw materials, that it lowered their standard of life, that it put them in a position of inferiority and so on. They say that Germany lacks "living space" or *Lebensraum*, although if you work it out there are less people to the square mile in Germany than there are in England or Belgium. And at the same time they say that the Germans are by nature a "master race" or *Herrenvolk*, and that they have been destined by divine Providence to seize the rich possessions of the "pluto-democracies" and to crush their weaker neighbours. We can, if we like, reply that all this is utter nonsense. That the Treaty of Versailles was not a brutal treaty and that, in fact, it was far more lenient than the treaties or conditions which Germany in the past and in the present has imposed upon her conquered enemies. We can say that the expression *Lebensraum* does not really mean "more living space" but "more loot." We can say that Germany was never deprived of raw materials, which she was always able to purchase in the open market. And we can point out that it is not very logical to complain at one moment that one is being bullied and ill-treated, and at the next moment to claim that as a *Herrenvolk* one has the right to bully and ill-treat.

3. The German Idea

We can say all this, but if we really wish to understand the German point of view, it does not get us very much farther. If a German were to say frankly what he feels he would, I imagine, express himself somewhat as follows: "We are a nation of more than eighty millions of people, situated in a central position in Europe, possessing a genius for warfare and capable of immense achievements of organisation and discipline. Owing to the misfortune of our history we have never been able to acquire that dominant position to which our manifest destiny entitles us. The older countries of the world have become soft and lazy and have ceased to believe in their own mission. We, as a young and ardent race, believe passionately in our own mission. It is a historical necessity that we should inherit the earth."

Were I a young German, trained in the Nazi school, I should regard such a statement as unanswerable. But as I am an elderly Englishman, trained in liberalism and the humanities, I do not regard it as unanswerable in the very least. I should answer it as follows: "If human society is to continue and to progress it can only do so under a system of law which gives equal rights and equal protection to strong and weak alike. You deny this simple truth and hold that might is always right. What you call the misfortune of your history is, in fact, the misfortune of your national character. By behaving as you have always behaved you arouse the hatred, and finally the armed hostility, of all law-abiding nations, and you end, in spite of your superb martial qualities, in being beaten. You will go on being beaten until you come to recognise the rule of law."

4. Force or Argument?

Essentially, therefore, this war has arisen because Germany believed that force was all-important, whereas we believed that law was so important that in order to defend law we must, in the last resort, ourselves resort to force.

It is important, when examining the actual circumstances which led to the present war, to bear this fundamental principle in mind. So long as Germany was seeking, by more or less legal means, to establish her own rights, the democracies treated her with careful, if at times mistaken, patience. But when it became absolutely clear that Hitler had no regard for law and believed only in violence, then we were forced, very much against our will, to resist him with his own weapons.

What, therefore, apart from this fundamental principle, were the circumstances or causes which brought about the Second German War?

II. "Ultimate" and "Immediate" Causes

It is never easy to give a simple explanation of the causes of great wars. Wars are like illnesses: you have a general condition of unfitness and then some tiny germ or microbe is able to conquer the whole body. It may, for instance, be true that a man got rheumatic fever because he was too lazy to change his socks; the fact that his socks were wet may well have been the "immediate" cause of his illness; but the "ultimate" cause was that his general condition was so poor that he had not the strength to throw off the illness from the start. In the same way wars have an "immediate" and an "ultimate." cause.

1. The Picture Out of Focus

If we concentrate our attention solely upon the *immediate* cause of this war, namely Hitler's attack upon Poland, we shall be apt to get the whole photograph out of focus, to blur its edges, and to allow the foreground to fade into the background. German propaganda seeks deliberately to create this confusion; they do not want us to get a clear picture of what really happened; they want our picture to be so indistinct and muzzy that we shall ask ourselves: "But what, after all, is this whole beastly business about?" Lord Haw-haw,* for instance, is constantly telling us that

---

* Lord Haw-Haw was the nickname most commonly associated with William Joyce, an American-born, Irish-raised, erstwhile British informant on the IRA, who broadcast Nazi propaganda (in English to the UK) from Germany during the war. Joyce was captured by the British in 1945 and, as he held a valid British passport during the period of his broadcasting, was executed for treason early in 1946. *Germany Calling: A Personal Biography of William Joyce, 'Lord Haw-Haw'* by Mary Kenny was published by New Island Books, Dublin, 2003.

all this suffering and destruction is due to the fact that the British Government refused to admit that the German city of Danzig should become part of Germany. By this means he concentrates attention upon the immediate causes of the present war and at the same time provides us with an account of those causes which is demonstrably untrue. This war is not being fought for Danzig; it is being fought because Hitler proved to the world that he was determined to overthrow the law of nations by violence.

2. The Immediate Cause: Poland

None the less the immediate cause of this war, namely the treaty rights of Poland, deserves examination. The issue has been much confused by clever propaganda on the German side and by vagueness, ignorance and forgetfulness on ours. For, in fact, the case of Danzig is not in the very least such as the Germans make out. It is not the case of a man seeking to assert his own just rights; it is the case of a man seeking by violence to suppress the just rights of others. Let me describe the exact circumstances.

3. How Poland was Remade in 1919

When, in the autumn of 1918, the German High Command realised that their whole front was crumbling and that the German armies were faced with the greatest defeat in history, they asked for an armistice. They promised, if the armistice were granted, to accept the Fourteen Points of President Wilson. Now Point 13 of this famous manifesto laid it down that Poland should "include territories inhabited by indisputably Polish populations and be assured free and secure access to the sea." The difficulty was that although there was a wide belt of territory running up to the Baltic the population of which was "indisputably Polish" within the meaning of Point 13, yet the city of Danzig, which was at the end of this corridor, was unquestionably a German and not a Polish city. Had Hitler been making the Peace Treaty we know very well what he would have done. He would have turned out the old inhabitants of Danzig and replaced them by new inhabitants, even as he has since ejected the Poles from Posen. The Paris Conference hesitated to take such drastic measures. The Poles were given the belt of indisputably Polish territory, subsequently called "the Corridor," and Danzig was made a free city under the League of Nations, and with full local protection for the German inhabitants. The point, however, is not whether the settlement made in 1919 of the Danzig question was a wise or an unwise settlement: the point is that on this matter at least the Germans cannot claim that the settlement was imposed upon them after they had surrendered, since in fact they had accepted this arrangement before they laid down their arms.

4. The Germans Begin to Eat Their Words and to Lie

During the years that followed the Germans conducted a very clever propaganda campaign, especially in this country, against the "Polish Corridor." They entirely forgot that they had promised before their surrender that Poland should have "free and secure access" to the sea, nor did they ever admit the fact that Danzig was being treated as a free city. They kept on repeating that East Prussia had been sundered from the rest of Germany, whereas, in fact, she had been far less sundered than Alaska is sundered from the United States or New Zealand from Great Britain. In spite of this, however, the Polish problem had begun to settle itself, and there seemed reason to hope, by 1930, that some further adjustment might be made such as would suit both Polish and German desires.

This hope was confirmed, somewhat to everybody's surprise, when Hitler seized power in 1933. On January 26th, 1934, as his first major diplomatic action, he signed a treaty with Poland under which the arrangement regarding Danzig and the Corridor was to remain in force for 10 years. On February, 1938, he informed the Reichstag that this agreement had "taken the poison out of the relations between Poland and Germany." "This dangerous spot," he added, "from the point of European peace has entirely lost its menacing character." He repeated this assurance in September, 1938; and so late as January, 1939, he proclaimed that "the friendship between Germany and Poland was one of the reassuring factors in the political life of Europe."

5. Hitler Exposes His Own Lie

There were many people in England who believed these assurances and who persuaded themselves that Hitler was, in fact, determined not to raise again the question of the Polish settlement. Other people were not quite so sure. There were those who had studied Hitler's methods and had observed his passion for doing one thing at a time, and for peeling the diplomatic artichoke leaf by leaf until only the choke remained. Such people contended that even as Hitler had lulled Europe into somnolence when he was seizing Austria, so also was he anxious to keep Poland quiet white he was engaged in swallowing Czechoslovakia. The predictions of these "scare-mongers" were rapidly fulfilled. On March 5th, 1939, Hitler, in violation of the Munich agreement, seized Prague. A week later (having got away with that robbery) he started on Poland. On March 21st, 1939, he informed the Polish Ambassador in Berlin that, in spite of his treaty of 1934, he must have Danzig and at once. The British Government by that time had become aware that Hitler was not merely seeking to redress his own wrongs but to violate the rights of others. On March 31st Mr. Chamberlain informed the House of Commons that although the British Government would welcome any settlement of the Polish question which might be come to by peaceful negotiations, yet if Hitler were to apply force to Poland, we should feel obliged "at once to lend Poland all support in our power." This meant, as it was intended to mean, that if Germany attacked Poland we should go to war.

6. Wheedling and Terrorising

Hitler can scarcely contend therefore that he was not given fair warning. Chamberlain had, in fact, said to him: "If you come to a fair agreement with Poland we shall be delighted; but if you start banging Poland about the head, then we shall be in it against you." In other words we warned Hitler that we should not allow him for the sixth time in six years to break the law of nations.

For a few weeks (but only for a few weeks) Hitler drew in his horns. He realised that this time we were in earnest and that we could not again be rocked to sleep by pretty promises. He therefore decided, since he could not wheedle us, to try to frighten us. He opened negotiations with Moscow, and on August 21, 1939, he startled the world with the German-Soviet agreement. On the very next day Mr. Chamberlain addressed to Hitler a letter of friendly warning. He told him that whatever the nature of the pact he had concluded with Russia our promises to support Poland if she were attacked still remained good. He pointed out to him that "war between our two peoples would be the greatest calamity that could occur." He went on to say that he did not believe that the Danzig question could not be resolved without the use of force and he offered to do anything within the power of the British Government to assist in a friendly solution. President Roosevelt added his appeal to that of Mr. Chamberlain. "I appeal to you," he wrote to Hitler, "in the name of the people of the United States, and I believe in the name of peace-loving men and women everywhere, to agree to a solution of the controversies existing between your Government and that of Poland." The Poles for their part made it abundantly clear that, whereas they were ready and anxious to accept a negotiation, they would not surrender to force. Hitler was deaf to all these appeals. On September 1, 1939, his troops invaded Poland. Two days later we were at war with Germany.

III. The Ultimate Causes. Hitler's Lawlessness

1. Was it our Business?

Such were the immediate causes of the Second German War. You may say: "But how can the ordinary man or woman be expected to understand all this diplomatic bargaining?" You may say: "I quite see that Hitler behaved trickily, but what I do not see is why that was any business of ours. Why, in other words, should we have risked the whole structure of the British Empire, and exposed our women and children to death from the skies, merely because of what Hitler did, or did not do, in a Baltic city of which many of us had never even heard?" You may say: "I admit that Hitler committed a crime against international order. But why should we have to be the policemen of Europe? We have the rule of law in our own country, but why should we seek to impose it, at great risk to ourselves, upon other countries?"

To your first question I should answer as follows: "You know very well that it is not a matter of diplomatic bargaining. You know very well that the point was whether Hitler could be trusted or not." "Yes," you may answer, "I admit that, but I still do not see why it was any business of ours. If I find that a man who is far stronger than I am cheats at cards, I do not risk a bad beating by hitting him in the face, I merely make a firm resolution never in any circumstances to play cards with that man again. We knew that Germany was almost twice as strong as we were. Why did we not disclaim all responsibility for Germany's actions, and pass by on the other side?" The answer is that four times we tried to walk away; the fifth time Hitler came running after us gnashing his teeth.

I must now leave the immediate causes of the war and pass to what is the second part of my argument, namely the ultimate causes of the war. In other words I must leave the foreground and examine the background.

2. Previous Acts of Lawlessness

The first point to understand is, as I have said, that we *did* try, again and again, to "pass by on the other side," to say that it was none of our business, and to believe the German propaganda to the effect that Germany had had a raw deal at Versailles (which is largely untrue) and that she was only struggling to regain "equality" and to assert her just rights. All this was wishful thinking and an evasion of our duty as a Great Power. Let me repeat that the war came to us, not because Hitler broke his treaties and promises regarding Danzig, but because he had done exactly the same thing four times already. I must at this stage give you a short catalogue of Hitler's major betrayals.

(a) **German Rearmament.** In the hope of preventing a Second German War the Treaty of Versailles laid it down that German forces by land, sea and air should not exceed a certain figure. In May, 1933, Hitler accepted this and said: "Germany will tread no other path than that laid down by the treaties." In October of that year Hitler walked out of the Disarmament Conference and the League of Nations and started to arm, both secretly and openly.

(b) **The Locarno Treaties.** The object of these Treaties, which were concluded many years after Versailles, was to prevent a conflict between France and Germany. They provided among other things that under no circumstances should either France or Germany send armed forces into the Rhineland. In January, 1934, Hitler said: "The German Government is ready to accept not only the letter but the spirit of Locarno." On March 7, 1936, Hitler violated these treaties and occupied the Rhineland with German forces.

(c) **Austria.** On May 21, 1935, Hitler said: "Germany neither intends nor wishes to interfere in the internal affairs of Austria, to annex Austria or to conclude the Anschluss." On March 11, 1938, Hitler annexed Austria by force.

(d) **Czechoslovakia.** On March 7, 1936, Hitler said: "We have no territorial demands to make in Europe. Germany has no desire to attack either Poland or Czechoslovakia." Having said these words he at once began to stir up trouble in the Sudetenland, using Conrad Henlein as his local agent. By September, 1938, his menaces became undisguised. We find him talking of "the reign of terror of the Bolshevik Hussite criminals in Prague." France was bound by treaty to come to Czechoslovakia's assistance if she were attacked, and it was obvious that if France intervened we also should be dragged in. Mr. Chamberlain therefore flew to meet Hitler and eventually the Munich Agreement was signed. Under this treaty Hitler obtained the Sudetenland but the rest of Czechoslovakia retained its independence. "I shall not," proclaimed Hitler, "be interested in the Czechoslovak State any more." On March 15, 1939, six months later, Hitler invaded Czechoslovakia, seized the capital and proclaimed the country a German protectorate.

3. What We Had Already Lost

It is clear from the above that even before he attacked Poland Hitler on four vital occasions had broken his promises and violated the treaties by which he was bound. By rearmament, by the occupation of the Rhineland, by the seizure of Austria and by the destruction of Czechoslovakia he had enormously increased the power and strategic might of Germany. In our dread of war, in our longing for peace, we had overlooked each one of these acts of spoliation, hoping against hope that once Hitler had gained his immediate objectives he would "become satisfied" and settle down to being a peaceful member of society. He did not settle down. After these four flagrant breaches of faith he made it clear that he was determined to commit a fifth breach; he meant to destroy and to annex Poland as he had destroyed and annexed the other countries on his borders. It was not, therefore, a question of whether Germany should or should not have Danzig; it was a question whether France and Great Britain could afford to hand over to Hitler the unchallenged mastery of Europe. We had already lost, not only the respect of the world, but our own self-respect, owing to our supine attitude on these four vital occasions. Had we swallowed the Polish violation as well, then we should have ceased for ever to have any further say in the destinies of Europe. About that there can be no question whatsoever.

War Was Thrust Upon Us

4. We Would Have Been Caught Anyhow

There are none the less some people who will persist in saying: "Yes, I admit that Germany is a ferocious country and that under Hitler she has run amok. But surely it would have been wiser for us to have remained out of the whole turmoil and to have sat quiet behind our own moat?" I doubt myself whether the British public would, in fact, have remained quiet once Hitler had established himself on the other side of the moat, and occupied all the European harbours from Narvik to Bordeaux. But that is not the point. The point is not so much whether we ourselves *wanted* to remain out, as whether Hitler would *allow* us to remain out. Take the case of Russia. The Soviet Government were determined (at any cost) to keep out of the war; they went so far as to enter into a Treaty of Friendship with Hitler a few days before he attacked Poland. But all these peaceful intentions were of no avail. Hitler, without even the semblance of an excuse, hurled his vast armies into an invasion of the Soviet Union. If Russia, who was bound to

Hitler by a treaty of non-aggression, was unable to avoid attack, how could we (a far smaller and more vulnerable nation) ever have hoped to remain immune from the fury of his malice and ambition? The idea is inconceivable.

5. And Then—

It may be unfortunate that we should be a small and overcrowded island dependent upon world trade for our existence; it would be much nicer to be a huge, self-contained unit such as Russia or the United States, or even a small self-contained unit such as Sweden or Denmark; but the fact remains that having a large population upon a very small island, we are dependent for our very life upon retaining command of the seas. In other words, the alternative is not one between being a large country or a small country, the alternative is between remaining a Great Power or ceasing to be a country at all. It is not sensible to say: "But what would it matter to me if Hitler did come, I should still have my old age pension." An old age pension in such circumstances would have the purchasing power of something less than 2d. a year.

6. War the Worst Evil?

In 1939 there were many people (even as to-day there may be a few people), who say: "That's all very well, but war is the greatest evil which man can commit. At any cost I shall refuse to go to war." It is as if they were to say: "Cancer is the worst of all human illnesses; from henceforward I pledge myself never to have cancer." Russia, Denmark, Norway, the United States, all hated the idea of war; they never made war; in the shape of Hitler it came to them.

The first answer, therefore, to the question "Why are we at war?" is, "Because we could not help it." But that is not by any means the only answer. For practical reasons we *could* not (however much we desired it) have kept out of this war. For moral reasons we *ought* not to have done so. I do not agree with those who say that war is the worst of all human miseries. I agree that it is *almost* the worst, but it is not *quite* the worst. The worst of human miseries is the triumph of evil. And if Hitler wins, then evil will have triumphed.

IV. The Moral Issue

It is customary in war-time for each side to represent the other side as the emissaries of the Evil One. I know the Germans very well, having at different times lived as much as six years in their country. I like the Germans and am not in the least ashamed of calling myself pro-German, even as I call myself pro-British, pro-American or pro-French. The Germans have great virtues and I do not regard them as masters of iniquity. But I do regard Hitler and his doctrine as the most evil doctrine ever invented by the mind of man. I regard it as the denial of all that humanity has discovered of good in the last 2,000 years.

1. Hitler the Destroyer

What do I mean by that? Let me explain. I am not a cynical person and I believe that mankind progresses slowly and surely towards perfection. The waves may ebb backwards and forwards, but the tide rises. Now if you examine that slow course of progression over the last 2,000 years you notice that there are certain stages in human advancement, or certain discoveries made or given to man, which guide him a step or two further towards his goal of perfection. Thus the Greeks discovered the beauty of the free mind searching after truth. The Romans discovered the importance of law and the sanctity of treaties and contracts. Christ came to us to teach us that God is love. The age of chivalry evolved the theory that the duty of the strong was to protect the weak. The French in the eighteenth century discovered the importance of reason and scientific thought, and we in England discovered that peculiar type of tolerance which we call "fair play." Consider, therefore, these six great stages of advance in human progress. Hitler denies all six of them, and not only does he deny them; he wishes to uproot them from human life. He does not believe in the free mind; he believes that men should only think or read or say what he tells them. He does not believe in truth; he has himself written of the importance of telling very big lies. He has broken every treaty, violated every promise into which he ever entered. He calls the Christian doctrine of love "a bourgeois inhibition." He has proclaimed openly that the duty of the strong is to glory in their strength and that the weak must be crushed into submission. He does not believe in reason and says that men should be guided only by their emotions and his own "somnambulist certainty." And he has no conception, no conception whatsoever, of what we mean by the phrase "fair play."

2. What We Are Fighting For

I said at the beginning of this article that once one could answer the question "*Why* are we fighting?" one got very near to answering the question "What are we fighting *for?*" I know very well myself what we are fighting for. We are in the first place fighting for our lives, since if Hitler wins we shall be starved to death even as the Greeks to-day are being starved. But we are also fighting for something more important than our lives. We are fighting for the things which mankind has discovered in the last 2,000 years. We are fighting to prevent the world surrendering to an evil doctrine of violence and untruthfulness. We are fighting evil things.

When, therefore, I am asked: "Why are we at war?" I answer as follows: "First, because there was no alternative between war and surrender. Secondly, because had we chosen surrender we should have exposed our people and future generations to disgrace and misery."

3. The Shape of Things to Come

These reasons satisfy me personally. I know that this war will deprive me for ever of many of the things which in the past gave me pleasure or comfort. But it will not deprive me (since we shall win this war) of the beliefs that I put higher than these selfish things. It will not deprive me of my belief in Great Britain, of my faith in human nature, of my conviction of human progress, of my sense of human values. That is enough for me, but it is not enough for everyone. After all, I am an elderly man, and the material world as I knew it will pass away. But younger people want something more than the preservation of the decencies of life, the preservation of the right of free speech and action, the preservation of law. They want a new world. They want a world of greater personal opportunity. They want a world free from poverty and fear. Well, they will get that new world, and in their own shape and not in Hitler's shape. And above all they will remember with pride and thankfulness that when all Europe bowed down to Moloch we in this little island maintained at great risk and at great sacrifice our independence, our courage, our unity, our good temper, our fairness and our faith.

March of Time: 1919 to 1939

Very few of us have got clear in our minds what happened between the two wars. This brief sketch may serve as a guide.

I. Period of Progress—1919-1926

THE Peace Treaties* were based on President Wilson's Fourteen Points, which Germany accepted. Germany evacuated Belgium and France, and restored Alsace-Lorraine, seized in 1871, and also, after a plebiscite, part of Slesvig taken from Denmark in 1864. Poland was reconstituted for the first time since her dismemberment by Austria, Prussia and Russia in the eighteenth century, and was granted a "corridor" to the sea west of Danzig, which, with Memel, was declared a free city under the League. Further, Germany handed over her colonies to the League, which "mandated" them to one or other of the victors. Out of Austria-Hungary, which had been breaking up before the armistice (November 11th, 1918), were set up the new state of Czechoslovakia; Hungary, much diminished by the loss of territory in Slovakia, East Hungary (to Rumania), Croatia and Slavonia; Austria; and Yugoslavia, which was built up from Serbia, Croatia, Slavonia, Bosnia and Montenegro. Now between Germany and Russia lay a sector of small refounded states from Estonia to Austria.

Germany was disarmed, being allowed only 100,000 long-service soldiers, plus police, no tanks, heavy guns or 'planes, and a

---

* With Germany: Versailles, June 28th, 1919; with Austria: St. Germain, September 10th, 1919; with Bulgaria: Neuilly, November 27th, 1919; with Hungary: Trianon, June 1st, 1920; with Turkey: Lausanne, July 23rd, 1923.

navy without large ships. This was to have been part of a general disarmament consistent with internal security, as stated by Wilson. At the Peace Conference, however, France demanded the left bank of the Rhine, but agreed to drop her claim on her frontiers being guaranteed by Wilson and Lloyd-George on behalf of their respective governments. Thus, when the U.S.A. refused to accept the Convention, in which refusal she was followed by the U.K.; and when further the U.S.A. would not join the League, France maintained her armaments, though the U.K. did not. This failure in general disarmament became one of Germany's standing grievances.

France relied largely upon economic pressure and the extraction of reparations to prevent the rearmament of Germany; and in pursuance of that policy, in January, 1923, occupied the industrial area of the Ruhr until August 1924. This action added to the bitter feeling already alive in Germany. There, as early as March, 1920, a military revolt against the German (Weimar) government, the Kapp *putsch* had revealed trouble, and in November, 1932, Ludendorff and Hitler produced the famous Munich *putsch*, the first outward sign of the Nazi idea. It failed, and Hitler was imprisoned.

In the meantime matters had been going badly in Germany, which together with some other European countries, had suffered badly from the economic chaos which followed the defeat of the Central Powers. The rise in the cost of living (the "inflation") in Germany was so steep that the mark, before the war worth about a shilling, declined rapidly in value from 1921, and, by October, 1923, it took 19,000 million marks to buy £1 worth of goods. This caused widespread misery; the savings of the middle-class vanished, creating a ruined section of society ready to take revenge on profiteers and working class when the moment came. In Italy (which, it should be noted, had been unsatisfied at the Treaty, and from the beginning cast eyes on the other Adriatic coasts), similar conditions led to the rise of the Fascist party under the ex-socialist Mussolini; in October, 1922, they seized power (the "march on Rome") and established a dictatorial regime.

Between 1919 and 1924 various agreements were entered into between the victorious Powers: the Nine-Power Pact to stabilise the Pacific and ensure a "hands off China" policy was signed in 1922, and in the same year the U.K., the U.S.A., Japan, France and Italy signed the Five-Power Washington Naval Treaty, in which the ratios of naval strength were to be 100, 100, 60, 35, 35. France entered into a number of agreements for mutual security with smaller countries such as Czechoslovakia, set herself to build up alliances in the Balkans, and eventually, in 1935, with Russia. Till 1925 Europe still seemed very unsettled, and fear was still dominant, but in that year the air cleared considerably thanks to the Treaty of Locarno, signed in December. In January of that year, Hindenburg had become President, implying that Germany was abandoning the social democracy of Weimar, and Stresemann, who stood for the "fulfilment of Versailles," had become Chancellor. The Treaty was largely a multilateral guarantee of frontiers, except the German eastern frontiers, though Germany promised not to go to war about them. In return for guarantees, evacuation of occupied territories took place earlier than under the Versailles Treaty, and Locarno was regarded as bringing about a new spirit, ushering in the real peace. Thus, when in the next year the Disarmament Preparatory Commission had its first session, it met with a confidence which was increased by the admission of Germany to the League.

For at this time it still seemed possible that the League might achieve its ends. It had helped to settle the problems of the Baltic States, and to rescue Austria and Bulgaria. It was doing useful work in suppressing certain international evils, such as the drug traffic, and America was beginning to take an interest in it, being shortly to join one of its most important sections, the International Labour Office. Now that most of the danger centres appeared to be calm, and the economic situation seemed to be clearing up, it looked as though the Treaties and the League between them might establish a durable peace.

II. Period of Confusion—1927–1934

But the next period was dominated by the "economic blizzard" which swept over the world, beginning in New York in 1929, and lasting till 1934. It made hopeless any attempt to settle the reparations question, these being finally abandoned at Lausanne in 1931. In June the next year, the World Economic Conference proved a complete failure, each country thenceforward becoming more and more inclined to economic nationalism. Attempts at agreement on disarmament failed as evidently as attempts at economic agreement. As early as 1927 the U.K. and the U.S.A, disagreed on naval limitation. In 1928 the U.S.A. announced a Big Navy programme, though in the same year 15 nations, including the U.S.A. and the U.S.S.R., signed the Kellogg Pact outlawing war. In 1931 Germany launched the pocket battleship *Deutschland*. In 1934, after the U.K. and Germany had both increased their defence estimates, the Disarmament Conference finally closed down and Japan denounced the naval limitation treaties she had signed at Washington in 1922 and in 1930. Japan's lack of interest in disarmament had, however, been made apparent in 1931 when she invaded Manchukuo,* at the height of the European economic crisis. This is often taken as marking the end of the peace, especially as the League, although condemning the aggression, failed to intervene.

It was in these years that the Nazis rose to power. Hitler published "Mein Kampf," and in 1930 the Nazis polled 6.4 millions at a general election, 18 per cent. of the electorate. At the Presidential election of 1932 Hindenburg polled 18.6 million votes, Hitler 11.3. In May of that year the Chancellor Bruening (whom we might class as "liberal") was replaced by Von Papen, indicating that

---

* i.e., Manchuria.

the Weimar Republic was nearing collapse. There were two general elections that year. July: Nazis, 229; Socialists, 121; Communists, 88. There was a slight swing back in November: Nazis, 196; Socialists, 121; Communists, 100. In January, 1933, however, Hindenburg made Hitler Chancellor; in February the Reichstag was burnt, and the Nazi terror began, Hindenburg in March giving Hitler dictatorial powers for four years. In September of that year Dolfuss became dictator in Austria, and in October Germany gave notice of her withdrawal from the League. In February, 1934, Austrian democracy came to an end with a massacre of socialists; in June, Hitler and Mussolini met for the first time, and soon afterwards occurred the notorious "blood bath" in which Hitler murdered his Nazi rivals. In July, Dolfuss was murdered by Austrian Nazis imported from Germany, and when Hindenburg died in August, Hitler was declared Fuehrer, a plebiscite showing that the Germans were 89 per cent. for him.

III. Period of Collapse—1935–1939

The Japanese seizure of Manchuria in 1931 was a forerunner of the other wars which were to be the curtain-raiser of the new world war. During this period the U.K. tried to follow out a policy of appeasement, which we can now see to have been hopeless. We began to rearm in a considerable way, though while the League was in existence, and France and ourselves were firm for peace, it was hoped to localise the quarrels. The preliminary wars began when in January, 1935, Italy started a frontier dispute with Abyssinia. The Emperor appealed to the League, but conciliation failed, and in November Italy declared war. The League decided to apply economic sanctions, but these broke down on the item of oil. A scheme devised by Sir Samuel Hoare and Laval was defeated by outraged British feeling, and both originators were forced to resign. Meanwhile, in March, Hitler defied the Versailles Treaty by introducing conscription and creating an air force. We protested, but after Germany, renouncing the disarmament clauses of Versailles, announced a new submarine programme, we made a new naval agreement with her, at which France protested.

In January, 1936, Dr. Goebbels announced: "We can do well without butter, but not without guns." In March, Hitler occupied the demilitarised Rhine zone with troops, again defying the Treaty of Versailles, and denounced Locarno. The Locarno Powers protested without effect, and elections in Germany showed the German people to be 99 per cent. pro-Hitler. In May, Mussolini announced the conquest of Abyssinia, and in July there broke out the Spanish civil war, which began as a rebellion against the Republic, set up after the revolution in 1931. In this war General Franco was strongly and officially aided by Germany and Italy, while the U.K. and France took up a position of non-intervention, in the hope of avoiding a conflict with the Axis powers, even denying the Spanish government its right to buy arms. By October the Axis had been established and, in November, Japan made an anti-Comintern pact with Germany.

The year 1937 is chiefly significant for the action of Japan in fanning local clashes into an invasion of China. China appealed to the League—as the Spanish government had done—but by this time the League was moribund. Japan refused mediation and, in November, Italy joined the anti-Comintern Pact.

During 1938 it became clear that war was, except for a miracle, bound to come. In January, there was a Nazi conspiracy in Vienna; in February, the Chancellor, Schuschnigg, was summoned to see Hitler; and in March, Germany took Austria over. Hitler said, "I have no further territorial ambitions." In April, the Sudeten Germans, a "minority" population in Czechoslovakia, began to agitate. France urged a compromise, and Lord Runciman went over from the U.K. to try to mediate. But matters became ever more threatening; and in August, Germany began to build the Siegfried Line. Early in September, the Sudeten leader saw Hitler; and, at a Nuremberg Nazi rally a few days later, Hitler made a provocative speech, after which France recalled her reservists. Negotiations went on; Germany rejected Czech proposals, and the Sudetens demanded self-determination, soon afterwards issuing a call to arms. On 19th [15th], Chamberlain visited Hitler at Berchtesgaden, as a result of which the U.K. and France suggested to the Czechs a peaceful transference of the Sudetenland. On 22nd and 23rd, Hitler, in another meeting with Chamberlain at Godesberg, made fresh demands, and it seemed that war was imminent. Hitler was told that the U.K., France and Russia were solid, and on 28th the British Navy was mobilised. But on 29th, Chamberlain again saw Hitler at Munich, together with Daladier, the French Prime Minister, and the Czechs, not present, were forced to hand over the Sudetenland. Hitler said: "I have no further territorial ambitions."

In March, 1939, Hitler invaded and took over the whole of Czechoslovakia, after which he declared "I have no further territorial ambitions," but at once occupied Memel. It was clear that the Munich agreement, "peace in our time," had been a blind, but no action was taken by the Powers. On April 1st, Franco triumphed, and the Spanish Republic, liberal in ideas, was replaced by a Fascist dictatorship. At Easter, April 7th, Italy invaded and took over Albania; and again no action was taken by the Powers, though in May the U.K. introduced conscription. As Nazi pressure became more and more insistent, the U.K. guaranteed Poland, Greece and Rumania against aggression, which could mean only that if either of these countries was invaded, the U.K. would declare war on Germany. This is what actually took place. After increasing aggressiveness in Danzig, in August the crisis became acute; and, on 23rd, Russia, to ward off immediate attack, signed a pact with Germany. On September 1st, Germany invaded Poland; on 3rd, after a final attempt to settle matters, England declared war on Germany at 11 a.m., to be followed a few hours later by France, and within a few days by all the Dominions.

WAR

What a Nazi Soldier Thinks

ABCA 'War' Pamphlet No. 24, August 8th, 1942, pp. 11-13

- *Another "Man You're Up Against" article—this time by an officer who has had contact with German prisoners in the Middle East.*

What a Nazi Soldier Thinks

UNTIL the German army met its match in numbers and weight of material after the onslaught against the Russian people, the German soldier was buoyed up by the consciousness of an unbroken series of swift, successful assaults in which countries toppled over like ninepins, and the aftermath of wine, butter, and silk stockings for the womenfolk at home seemed like a foretaste of the millennium for the "master-race."

That was the mood in which the German Africa Corps came to Libya in the spring of 1941. The youths who volunteered for service in Africa were tempted by stories of the lure of the mysterious continent. They were shown pictures of palm trees and of dusky beauties, were given a smart uniform to wear, and promised colonial allowance with leave home every three months.

Disillusionment was not long in coming. The dusky beauties were rare and out of reach. There was an inexplicable lack of palm trees, with clusters of dates and cooling shades, in the desert. There was too much sand. The leave promised at the end of three months did not materialise. Furthermore, the troops were plagued with the normal unpleasantness of the desert, including "Gyppy tummy," desert sores and sandflies.

Older Men Came

Yet, though there was a fair amount of grousing, this was not serious, and prisoners of war almost unanimously refused to admit that conditions were bad. Apart from a number who arrived still suffering from diarrhoea, or Gyppy tummy—and Germans are in any case subject to stomach trouble, which is their national malady—they were a healthy lot, and as they always took every opportunity to go about as nakedly as possible (unlike the Arab, who swathes himself in enveloping garments) they were mostly deeply sunburnt all over.

The majority were no more than 23 years of age, some much younger, but in the autumn reinforcements of older men began to arrive, men of from 35 to 45, some of whom had served in the French Foreign Legion. They all, young and old, replied to the request for the name of their unit with the stereotyped phrase: "I am a German soldier and am not allowed to say anything." Some of the younger and more recently arrived soldiers were mere boys of 18, who had volunteered at the age of seventeen. One of the older N.C.O.s replied: "I have had 20 years' service in the army and you cannot expect me to talk."

It was interesting and instructive to observe, during formal conversation with these men, how the Nazi regime had succeeded in moulding their minds in the same rigid, unthinking pattern.

A youth of 22 years of age had by 1941 lived for nearly nine years under the Nazi regime, i.e., since he was 12 years old. Even before that he had probably come under the influence of the Hitler Youth organisation.

Religion of Nazi-ism

The Fuehrer is for them a mythological figure appertaining to a god on earth. It was suggested early this year to a German officer that Hitler's last two speeches had appeared to reveal signs of incipient megalomania. A look of shocked horror spread over the officer's countenance as he protested: "You *really* must not say a thing like that to a German! He will be frightfully offended!"

Nazi-ism is, in fact, a religion, and the Nazi State is a religious State. We should regard it as a religion of Satan, but it is a religion none the less. Romanticism in decay tends to degenerate into Satanism, and that helps to explain the hold of Nazi-ism on the essentially romantic Germans.

So convinced is the German to-day that his political theory and philosophy are right, that he cannot understand why the British continue to resist the invincible might of Germany. The explanation he has found for himself is that Mr. Churchill is responsible for our British stubbornness, and that if only we would get rid of our present Prime Minister all would be well. He will not believe that Mr. Churchill incorporates the spirit of Britain as Hitler incorporates the spirit of Germany.

"Churchill," he says, "with the support of the Jews, has forged his yoke on the British people. Overthrow Churchill's baneful influence, and you and we will soon reach agreement. You will give us back our colonies, pay an indemnity to Germany for the trouble you have caused us, and leave Europe to us. In return, we shall leave you unmolested in your little island, which does not really belong to Europe, and you will of course in future restrict yourselves to no more than the share of world trade which is adequate for a small nation only half the size of ours."

No Sense of Justice

It is no good talking to a Nazi about justice, or ideas of justice. His views on this subject differ so radically from ours, that for all practical purposes it may be said that he has no sense of justice. The Germans have the inborn right, by virtue of being German, to perform actions—or as we should think, perpetrate crimes—which they deny others the right to perform. The Germans possess privileges, by right of being Germans, which other peoples do not possess. This is a tenet of faith and admits of no argument.

As one young German officer put it: "We are a people who must expand." Another officer, of a higher social class than the one just quoted, expressed the conviction that England would be invaded and the invasion would be successful. When it was suggested to him that every woman and child in this country would be armed in such an eventuality, he replied: "No! I don't believe that the English would arm women and children. The English are too fair-minded to do such a thing." He made it clear that in such a case the estimation in which he held the English gentleman would suffer a severe blow.

Failure is "Treachery"

Germans captured in Crete and the Western Desert were so filled with belief in their invincibility that when anything went wrong with their plans they frequently attributed it to "treachery." They were unable to explain what they meant by this, except that their intentions must in some way have been revealed to the enemy. This seemed to them a plausible explanation, and they did not try to analyse the situation any further.

Such mental inertia is typical of the lack of will on the part of the young German of to-day to think for himself. He does not, in fact, regard the capacity for independent thought as a desirable human quality. He and his comrades nearly all have this in common, that they will put forward the same, continually recurring arguments when justifying Germany's behaviour.

"Arguments" is, perhaps, too complimentary a term. They present not arguments, but catch-phrases, or slogans, which their mentors have imprinted on their minds in the process of "education" to which all Germans have been submitted. And if they are asked to explain or justify one catch-phrase, they will do so by merely quoting another.

The German soldier in Africa is more insulated against an understanding of the real position than is his fellow in Europe, and in the ignorance of present-day German youth lies the High Command's hope that the crumble in morale will not begin with the young soldier.

CURRENT AFFAIRS

The Development of Nazism

ABCA 'Current Affairs' Pamphlet No. 29,
October 24th, 1942

NAZI GERMANY

THE article by Dr. Aris in this number is written from the inside. It shows you the Nazis as they were; as they are; and as they always will be—until the disease is finally cured. It rubs in the essential point, viz., that, for the Nazis, the end always justifies the means, any means. Questions of right or wrong, of truth or falsehood, in our sense of the words, simply do not arise. If any action appears likely to produce an advantage then it would be folly to allow what we should call morality, decency or fairplay to stand in the way of it. The test of falsehood, in the Nazi mind, is not whether it is, in fact, falsehood, but whether it is likely to be believed by those to whom it is addressed. If it is likely to be believed, or if it would be advantageous, that it should be believed, then go ahead.

This means that the Nazi leaders have, and can have, nothing but the most complete contempt for those whom they have deluded. Have you ever watched the faces of Hitler and his associates on the films as one of their big parades marches by? It is enlightening. When they send Germans to the slaughter by the hundred thousand in Russia they are giving them precisely the fate which, from the Nazi point of view, they have deserved. They, or the great majority of them, were willing to be coerced like sheep, and now they meet the sheep's end.

This is the "evil thing" which we are fighting now, a vast system of mass-hypnotism, based always on the scientific: exploitation of the darkest sides of human nature and supported by organised brutality and ruffianism because only brutes and ruffians could do the dirty work. And, if you have sufficient brutes and ruffians, the rest do not count. "It never troubles the wolf how many the sheep may be."

When you explain to your men just what Nazism really means, and how long it has been developing, you will, in all probability, be asked this question: "Why, if this is true—and there is no reason to believe it is not—did we, and the other democratic nations, wait so long before calling a halt to Hitler and his gang?" The answer is that people always believe, as long as they possibly can, what they want to believe. The great majority of people in this country, right up to Munich, simply could not grasp the reality of organised evil in Germany. They did not want to believe that any European nation could be so hag-ridden.

It is essential to be absolutely frank about this. If we do not admit the real truth, viz., that we were, most of us, deceived, because we deceived ourselves for so long, then the suspicion will arise that there must have been a considerable body of people in this country then who hoped for advantage themselves from Hitler's victory and that this body still exists to-day. Any such supposition would be not only untrue but absolutely fatal to the unity which we need now and shall need after the war. We were, in fact, deceiving ourselves, hoping for the best without facing the worst. Now we, all of us, know the real truth, because we have no longer the slightest excuse for not knowing it. It is because democracy, instead of being merely an "article of issue," is now desperately fighting for its life, that we know what we mean when we say that "government of the people, by the people, for the people shall not perish from the Earth."

Books on Germany

Nordic Twilight, by E. M. Forster. (Macmillan War Pamphlets, 1940), 3d.

Germany's New Order, by Duncan Wilson. (Oxford Pamphlets, 1941), 4d.

Mein Kampf, by R. C. K. Ensor. (Oxford Pamphlets, 1939), 4d.

The Nazi Conception of War, by Walter J. Jones. (Oxford Pamphlets, 1940), 4d.

Labour Under Nazi Rule, by W. A. Robson. (Oxford Pamphlets, 1940), 4d.

National Socialism and Christianity, by N. Micklem. (Oxford Pamphlets, 1940), 4d.

The Gestapo, by O. C. Giles. (Oxford Pamphlets, 1940), 4d.

What Hitler Wants, by E. O. Lorimer. (Penguin, 1939), 9d.

One Man Against Europe, by K. Heiden. (Penguin, 1939), 9d.

Lies as Allies or Hitler at War, by Viscount Maugham. (Oxford University Press, 1941), 6d.

German Youth and the Nazi Dream, by E. V. Hartshorne. (Oxford University Press, 1941), 6d.

Germany, Then and Now, America Faces the War Series. (Oxford University Press, 1941), 6d.

Hitler Wants the World, by H. Rauschning. (Hurricane Books, 1941), 6d.

Germany Puts the Clock Back, by Edgar Mowrer. (Penguin, 1937), 9d.

That Bad Man, by Wickham Steed. (Macmillan, 1942), 5/-.

The House That Hitler Built, by S. Roberts. (Methuen, 1938), 5/-.

The Development of Nazism

Germany Economy, 1870-1940, by G. Stolper. (Allen and Unwin, 1940), 7/6.

Education for Death, by Gregor Ziemer. (Constable, 1942, 7/6.)

Germany's Revolution of Destruction, by H. Rauschning. (Heinemann, 1939), 10/6.

Hitler Speaks, by H. Rauschning. (T. Butterworth, 1939), 10/6.

Berlin Diary, 1934-1941, by William T. Shirer. (T. Hamilton, 1941), 12/6.

Mein Kampf, by A. Hitler, translated by Murphy (Thurston Blackett, 1939), 10/6.

The Fall of the German Republic, by R. T. Clark (Allen and Unwin, 1935), 15/-.

Dictatorship: Its History and Theory, by A. Cobham (Cape, 1939), 12/6.

British Survey, (3d.).—Vol. 1. No. 6. Germany: Policy and Opinion, 1939.

Vol. 1. No. 7. Germany: Economic Conditions.

Vol. 2. No. 4. How a Nazi is Made.

Read the heavy type only to get an abbreviated version of this article.

The Development of Nazism

By Dr. R. Aris, Full Time Lecturer to H.M. Forces

1. A Revolution That Was Not a Revolution

ON November 9th, 1918, the German sailors mutinied in Kiel Harbour. Like wildfire the revolt spread through the whole of Germany, the Emperor fled to Holland and Bismarck's second Reich collapsed. A few days later Germany sued for armistice. **The revolt of November, 1918, however, was not a real revolution** such as England experienced when Charles I was beheaded or as France did when Louis XVI lost his life. In a real revolution the whole form of the life of a nation is changed, but **in Germany things remained very much as they were.** It is true that the Kaiser disappeared from the scene and with him all the princes and princelings of Germany, but **the power of the industrialists,** the big steel magnates such as Krupp and Stinnes, **remained unbroken** and the **militarists waited** in the background **until their turn would come again.**

The Germans are not very good at revolutions and it is a curious fact that **a popular movement has never succeeded in Germany**. If it had, the whole course of history would have been altered and this country would not have had to fight Germany a second time during our lifetime. **The Germans**, as their leader Bismarck tells us, lack the quality of "civic courage," that is to say, however good they are as soldiers against external enemies, they **never dare to**

oppose their own government even when it is as criminal as was that of the Kaiser.

2. The Reichswehr

The new government was decidedly weak, composed as it was of men who **had no practical experience** of government and who were afraid of breaking the power of the reactionary forces in Germany. Although the heads of the administrative departments changed, their personnel remained largely the same, and most of the judges and teachers were hostile to the Republican government.

From the beginning of its existence the new government had to fight those radical sections of the German Labour Movement which were opposed to democracy and wanted to set up a Soviet regime in Germany after the Russian pattern. Riots and street fights all over Germany were the consequence and the government had to call in the soldiers in order to maintain peace. Thus at a critical moment in its existence **the Republican government became dependent on the army and remained so** until the end of the Weimar Republic. The centre of gravity in Germany, therefore, was not the government but the army, the Reichswehr as it was called after its reorganisation immediately after the end of the last war.

According to the Treaty of Versailles the German army was restricted to a hundred thousand officers and men, who had to be volunteers enlisting for a period of 12 years. This restriction, which was meant to curb German militarism, had a somewhat unforeseen result. **The men who volunteered for the Reichswehr** mostly came from the class which had supported the militarism of the Kaiser and **were definitely hostile to the new regime.** They were men who were keen on military service and who were longing for the day when Germany could try once again to conquer the world. **Their officers were still drawn from the same class** of noblemen and particularly from that section which we call the Prussian Junkers, who had provided the Kaiser with his best military leaders, even if it is true that sometimes, as in the case of Ludendorff, they did not belong to that class.

Perhaps you will have noted that almost all the German army leaders who have distinguished themselves in the present war are officers of the Reichswehr and have usually a "von" in front of their name, which denotes that they belong to the nobility. **All these men had taken an oath** that they would defend the constitution of the Weimar Republic with all its guarantees of personal freedom, **but they never took that oath very seriously** and they supported the Republican government only very half-heartedly and with many secret reservations. **They considered the Republic as a necessary evil** forced upon Germany by the Allies and to be overthrown as soon as there seemed to be a chance for a second World War.

Although **the Reichswehr** was not allowed to have aeroplanes, tanks and heavy guns, it **soon became** a highly trained and well disciplined military instrument and **the centre of real political power in Germany**, where the army has always played a very important part in politics. It soon became clear to every observer of German politics that **the fate of the Republic was** not **to be decided** by the majority of the German people, who, in fact, supported it, but **by the generals of the Reichswehr**, who often quite openly showed their contempt for it. As long as they considered the Republic as a useful smoke-screen behind which they could carry out their sinister game of secret rearmament, the Republic government was safe. On the day on which they decided to come out into the open with their policy of aggression and of total mobilisation of Germany's vast military power, the Republic was doomed.

3. Hitler Appears on the Scene

Adolf Hitler's military career was not particularly distinguished. He remained a lance-corporal during the four years of the war, and

The Development of Nazism

it is not exactly clear how he got the Iron Cross First Class, which is the only decoration he wears. When the Revolution broke out he was in a military hospital in North Germany, suffering from the after-effects of a British gas attack which had temporarily blinded him. It is still an unsolved mystery who was responsible for the appointment of this obscure young man as political officer, in which capacity he lectured extensively to German troops. From the account he gives us of his career in his book, there is no doubt that he **viewed the revolution from the beginning as a disaster for Germany** and that he considered the new government as a set of criminals. It throws a curious light on the powerlessness of the new government that it could do nothing to prevent this foreigner—for Hitler was not even a German subject—from carrying out his anti-republican propaganda. It was during this period that Hitler met **a group of fanatics** in a small beerhouse in Munich, where they used to hold political meetings discussing the future of Germany. They **had founded a new party which Hitler joined** as member No. 7, and which was the nucleus of **the National Socialist German Workers' Party**, the future Nazi Party.

4. The Cry for the Traitor

The men whom Hitler joined in Munich were fanatical cranks with very woolly ideas about life and politics, but with a burning hatred for the Treaty of Versailles, the new government and the Jews. When Germany collapsed, the German people felt stunned and could not understand what had happened. For four years they had celebrated victory after victory, for four years they been told that the German armies were invincible, after four years of war Germany had conquered the greater part of Europe and yet almost over-night, without any warning to the general public, the whole gigantic war machine came crashing down. The Germans could not understand that Germany could not stand up to the superior industrial resources of the United States and Great Britain and had simply exhausted herself and so, as it will always happen in circumstances like these, people began to look for treachery. It is a common human weakness that people try to fix the blame on somebody else if they fail to achieve their aim and the fanatics in Munich took advantage of this fact. **According to them Germany was not militarily beaten but was betrayed, stabbed in the back by the Jews, the Freemasons, the trades unions, and the "November criminals."** Of course **this was an enormous lie**; Germany was soundly beaten in the field in the autumn of 1918, but nevertheless quite a few people believed **the fairy-tale of the traitors**, which did not hurt their self-respect quite as badly as the grim realisation that the arrogant and over-confident German war lords had been beaten at their own game. In all his subsequent speeches, Hitler has again and again insisted on this misrepresentation of historical truth, and **the young Nazi of to-day is completely convinced that Germany would have won the war last time if it had not been for the Jew's. The older ones** are not quite so sure, because they still remember the terrible losses which Germany suffered before Verdun and in the Battle of the Somme, but they also **have deluded themselves into the belief that Germany cannot be beaten again.**

5. The Jews

The Jews have always been useful scapegoats and whipping-boys in times of trouble. Having been excluded for centuries from most professions, they **usually concentrated in the few trades that were left open to them** and they acquired wealth and influence, sometimes out of proportion to their numbers in the countries in which they lived. The German Jews were on the whole law-abiding and loyal citizens, who played their part in Germany's war effort and who suffered equally with other Germans from the effects of Germany's defeat. Jews had contributed much to Germany's economic and financial development and quite a few of Germany's leading scientists were of Jewish race. **In times of trouble**, however, **hatred can easily be directed against them**, particularly as individual members of their community react against centuries of persecution in such a way as to give the Jew-baiter material for his anti-Jewish propaganda. It was also true that there were a number of Jews among the leaders of the revolutionary movement in Germany, and as there had always been an anti-Semitic tradition in Germany, it was not difficult to stir up hatred against them, particularly among the middle classes.

6. Nazism and the Middle Classes

Fascism has often been called the revolt of the middle classes. The little man, the black-coated worker, the small trader, the professional in all countries felt deeply insecure after the last war. They felt dimly that they were being crushed between the two millstones of Capital on the one hand and organised Labour on the other. They noticed that they were squeezed out of business by the big combines and chain stores without being able to fight for their rights in the way the workers could with their organised trades unions. In Germany the middle classes had always been particularly loyal citizens and had provided the German army with good soldiers and non-commissioned officers and the German government with hard-working Civil Servants. To them the collapse of the Second Reich came as a severe shock, since they were to suffer particularly severely from the economic crisis which was the result of the war in almost all the countries which had been involved in it. It was not very difficult to make use of their resentment and bitterness and to foment in them a sense of being wronged which, in its turn, gave place to a fierce and burning nationalism, especially among the younger generation, to whom the impoverished Republic could offer very little by way of jobs or by way of excitement. **It was among the middle classes that anti-Semitism found its most ardent supporters.** The Jews, mostly belonging to the middle classes themselves, were very likely to come up against the members of their own class **as competitors in the economic field** and in times of crisis competition tends to lead to friction and hatred, particularly if one group of the competitors is so characteristically different from the rest as in the case of the Jews.

7. The Inflation

During all wars and immediately afterwards we always notice inflationary tendencies. Prices begin to rise and the purchasing power of money falls. In Germany this process was carried out to its bitter end and by 1923 1,000 milliard marks were worth one shilling. There is no doubt that **the Government could have prevented this complete collapse of the German currency** if it had carried out a policy of control of prices and wages and had forced the people to save. **The industrialists, however,** who by 1922 had already gained considerable influence over the government, **welcomed the Inflation as a means of getting rid of their own obligations**, and they also hoped that the complete collapse of Germany's economic life would convince the Allied leaders of the folly and uselessness of reparations.

The consequences of **the Inflation** were far-reaching and disastrous. It **meant nothing more or less than the complete destruction of the economic power of the middle classes**, who suffer most in an inflation. The industrialists and landowners did not fare so badly, as their factories and their land retained their value, the workers did not suffer so much, as their savings had been small and as their wages were increased in proportion as prices rose, but the middle classes lost all their savings and were economically completely ruined. Although the Jews as a class suffered just as severely, individual members of the Jewish community managed to weather the storm better than the others, as they had more financial experience and realised more clearly what was happening. This of course was grist to the mill of the anti-Semites, and it was **from the ruined and disillusioned middle classes** that **German Fascism drew most of its first recruits.** Most of the Nazi leaders come from this class and it is certainly no overstatement to say that

without the Inflation Hitler would never have got into power.

8. What Is Nazism?

Fascism, although it took its most virulent form in Germany, is not a German invention, and we find it in different forms in many countries. We have already shown that it is a movement with its roots in the middle classes, but it is more than that: it is the outcome of a gigantic social and moral crisis in the midst of which we are living. For many years a number of thinkers have been deeply critical of our social conditions, which they have attacked from different angles. Karl Marx taught that Capitalism was bound to develop into Socialism, and the leaders of the Russian Revolution were deeply inspired by his ideas. But Marx completely ignored the middle classes, which according to him should have joined the workers, but who in reality developed a new philosophy of their own in answer to Socialism. The middle classes were frightened of Socialism and could not see in the Russian ideology a solution for their own troubles. **Fascism,** therefore, **is a movement of the middle classes reacting against Communism. Hitler,** as is well known, has always **skilfully used this fear of Communism** and owes much of his success to it.

There are **many people** who **say that Nazism** is nothing new in Germany, that it **is simply a new form of Teutonic aggressiveness.** It is quite true that there have always been thinkers in Germany who have advocated very much the same things as Hitler does now, but it is more than probable that these ideas would never have won such a success had there been no inflation or huge unemployment. Many of the ideas which Hitler presents in his book are not of German origin. The racial theory, for example, was developed by Houston Stewart Chamberlain and Count Gobineau. According to this theory there is one specially gifted race, the Nordic race, in Europe, which is destined to rule the world. **The Germans claim to represent** that chosen race, and the feeling of belonging to a "Herrenvolk," **a master-race**, has given them much consolation at the time of their deepest humiliation, and makes them such arrogant and unbearable masters whenever they appear as conquerors. **The racial theory**, like so many of the Nazi ideas, **is from a scientific point of view utter nonsense** and is not supported by a single serious anthropologist outside Germany, but nevertheless it proved very useful propaganda in the hands of the Nazis.

Hitler's chief idea, indeed his only one, **is his belief in force.** He is convinced that life and the history of whole nations are determined by force alone. **According to him, wars** are not only inevitable, they **are necessary**; in wars nations become great, in eternal peace they would always decay. This idea is by no means new and many a thinker has expressed it, but it was left to Hitler and his collaborators to develop its consequences to the full. If you read his book, which is now available in a complete and faithful English translation, you will find that in all its pages there is not a trace of humour or kindliness, but only bitterness, hatred, and the belief that the bully carries the day. **The individual counts for nothing, he is simply a part of the all-powerful state**, and he must submit unquestioningly and completely to the orders of the leaders who claim to represent that state. Hitler contemptuously brushes aside all the attempts made by great leaders throughout history to replace the rule of force by the rule of law, and pours scorn on such an ideal as that of justice.

9. Hitler's First Putsch

In November, 1923, Hitler made his first bid for power. Although he had given his word of honour not to attempt to overthrow the legal government, he **started a revolt in Munich** in that theatrical way which made him for a long time the laughing-stock of the world, but appealed so much to many Germans. **The Putsch failed**, however, since the Reichswehr had not deemed the time had yet come **and Hitler was arrested** and put into prison, where he wrote the first volume of his book.

In prison Hitler had ample time for reflection, and it seems that **he thoroughly grasped the reasons for his dismal failure. He realised that** under modern conditions, with the vast accumulation of mechanical power in the hands of the government, the revolutionary who wants to acquire power must change his tactics. To use a modern military term, instead of undertaking a frontal attack **he must employ the tactics of infiltration.** Hitler took advantage of the weakness of **democracy**, which **allows anybody to canvass support for his ideas**, even if that person quite openly declares his intention to destroy the very foundations of democracy once he has acquired power. Thus **the Nazis**, in spite of their contempt for Parliamentarian tactics, **began** to send their representatives into Parliament and to gain support by a very simple device: **by promising everything to everybody.** To the peasants they promised high prices for their foodstuffs, to the workers they promised high wages and low prices for food, to the industrialists they promised rearmament and the destruction of the trades unions, to the middle classes they promised the abolition of interests and the dissolution of the chain stores and big trusts. **And all the time they played on German nationalism and on the anti-Semitic tendencies of the German middle classes.**

10. The Private Armies

Hitler realised that militarist tradition was very strong in Germany and appealed to almost all classes, but he also knew that a party which had at its disposal a well-disciplined group of men, trained on military lines, would be in a very strong position in the internal struggle for power. He **decided**, therefore, **to build up** a private army, or rather **two armies with definite functions. Captain Ernst Roehm**, one of the most unpleasant products of National Socialism, **was entrusted with the task of turning the riff-raff of the nation into** an army. For this purpose the money given by the industrialists was freely spent and many thousands of young men were given uniforms and were even paid some pocket money.

To many German youths the entry into **the Brown Army** was a pleasant escape from the misery of unemployment, and their little pocket money came in very handy, but quite a few joined the "brown battalions" because being Germans they loved uniforms and military parades and were quite content to leave all the thinking to their leaders. It is often not realised that in times of economic and social trouble people find it very difficult to think out their own problems and are only too glad if somebody promises them that he will do all the thinking for them.

In Germany this tendency was particularly strong as the Germans have always been used to obey their governments blindly and unquestioningly.

The Brown Army was employed **as a sort of bodyguard for the Nazi leaders** and was trained to break up and terrorise political meetings of their opponents. Undoubtedly **the many bullies who had enlisted in that army** got a lot of fun out of this kind of activity, and **gathered valuable experience** for the time when the victims of their terror were no longer only German Socialists, Catholics or Jews, but Poles and Czechs and other "inferior" races.

Apart from the Brown Army **the Nazis created another army,** the "Black Guards," now more commonly known as **the SS.** If the Brown Shirts were composed of the unemployed riff-raff, their black-shirted colleagues were **extremely carefully picked and trained specimens,** the cream of the bullies, so to speak, and **they were meant to be the military backbone of the Party. To-day** they have their own air force and panzer divisions and are stationed all over Germany to guard the Home Front. Wherever they appear **they are the terror of the population**, and many Germans are just as frightened of them as are the people in the conquered countries. They don't wear the skull and cross bones on their caps for fun; they would not hesitate to murder their own mothers if they were ordered to do so.

Public opinion abroad did not take these private armies very seriously for a long time. Their military value was considered not to be very high, but although it is true that until 1933 they were not very effectively armed, they formed a very powerful instrument in Germany's internal struggle and they helped to keep military tradition alive. That is why they were appreciated even by the leaders of the Reichswehr, although there always tended to be a certain jealous rivalry between the regular forces and the Party armies.

11. The Economic Crisis 1929-1933

For quite a number of years **the Nazis** remained a comparatively unimportant minority, although they were a constant source of trouble to the Republican authorities. **In 1928 they only polled 600,000 votes** in the whole of Germany, but many influential men secretly sympathised with them and the legal government was powerless in view of the support which the Nazis received even from members of the judiciary. In 1929 one of the worst economic storms ever experienced broke out in America, and Germany, like almost all countries, was plunged into another crisis. **Unemployment rose until in 1932** between six and seven million people, about a quarter of the working population, was receiving dole or public assistance. Three of the most important banks and one of the largest insurance companies collapsed and the result was that **the German people became panicky and quite demented.** Radicalism at both ends of the political scale grew and assumed alarming proportions. **In 1931 the Nazis polled 6,000,000 votes**, becoming the second strongest party, and **in 1932** in the elections for the Presidency **Hitler was supported by nearly 14,000,000 Germans.** The sands of the Republic were fast running out and nothing but **unity among the anti-Fascist forces** and speedy economic recovery could save it. Unfortunately, such unity **did not exist**, and when economic recovery was round the corner in 1932 it was too late, Germany was in the grips of a political fever which the sickly Republic could not survive.

12. Hitler Assumes Power

In January, 1933, Hitler was appointed Chancellor of the German Reich. His tactics had proved successful, he had attained power by constitutional means without having to resort to open force. In reality he owed his appointment to a sinister intrigue concerning which we have not yet got all the facts. **The reactionary forces in Germany**, the industrialists, the big land-owners and the Junkers, **persuaded Hindenburg to appoint the "Bohemian Corporal" because they realised they could use him to gain public support for their regime and they hoped to keep the unruly upstart whom they despised and distrusted in check.** But whatever history will have to say of Hitler it will not accuse him of attempting half measures. **Hitler wanted the reality of power**, and not merely its shadow, even if for the time being for tactical reasons he contented himself with sharing this power with others. This was quite in keeping with his theory of infiltration and his technique of defeating his enemies one by one when he thought their turn had come, very much in the same way in which he later was to act in the sphere of foreign politics. **A few months after he had taken over he arranged for a general election, but although the Reichstag building was set on fire to whip up the German people the Nazis did not secure a majority. Hitler then dissolved the Communist Party and the rest of the Reichstag granted him extraordinary and dictatorial powers.**

13. The Party

In democratic states parties are voluntary organisations of men and women who combine in order to achieve certain political aims. The Nazi Party is of a very different character and it is not very easy to define exactly what it is. For one thing **there is only one party in the country, and the elections which are held from time to time are really a farce as nobody can vote for anybody else but the official party candidates.** Not everybody can join the organisation, but only those who are considered politically reliable, and they have to submit to a very strict discipline. In this respect the Nazi Party resembles an army, and as in an army, there are a number of ranks in it, from the simple party member to the Commander-in-Chief. On the other hand, anybody who wants a job of any importance must be a member of the party and the fattest jobs are given to those who have been longest in the party. The party is supposed to be the centre of power in Germany, but **in reality of course power is in fact in the hands of a very small group of men who direct the party machine.** The party which, in democratic states, is outside the state, in Germany became identified with it.

14. Who Controls Whom?

It has often been suggested, particularly in the early stages of the Nazi Revolution, **that Hitler was only a figurehead** and that power really was in the hands of the army. That **was undoubtedly true at the beginning, when Hitler was the tool of the Reichswehr.** Even **in 1934 the army leaders were strong enough to force Hitler to carry out the drastic purge of June 30th when more than 1,000 Nazi leaders, among them Roehm, were killed. But very soon Hitler's tactics of infiltration secured his own position so strongly that nobody dared to oppose him.** His agents were everywhere and the Gestapo set up a network of spies all over Germany so that no serious opposition could develop from any quarter. **To-day** there is little doubt that **Hitler and a very small group of men**, among whom the most formidable is Himmler, the head of the Gestapo, **control the fate of Germany absolutely and dictatorially, even if the technical conduct of military operations is in the hands of professional soldiers.** And it would be sheer folly to believe that **the German people** are opposed to this dictatorship; there is, on the contrary, plenty of evidence that they **support it and will go on doing so until their military machine has been destroyed.**

15. Propaganda

Few people in this country quite realise what propaganda means in **Nazi Germany**. Like most things to which Hitler has turned his hand it **is organised on a totalitarian basis**, that is to say, **during his whole life the German citizen is subjected to an immense propaganda barrage from which there is no escape.** The aim of **this propaganda** is quite openly admitted; it **is intended to influence the mind of every German so that it works along certain rigidly prescribed lines.** He must become fanatically convinced of the superiority of the German race, and must be filled with an ardent desire to serve his leaders in their nefarious struggle for world domination. There is no education in Germany in the sense in which we understand it; **the German propagandists are not concerned with making their people think, but on the contrary with preventing them from thinking for themselves.** Education in the proper sense appeals to reason, it is meant to enable the pupil to choose between different alternatives which he has critically examined and thought out; **the propagandist in the Nazi sense** appeals to emotions and **tries to convince his victims that only one course of action is right, and that it is treason to think that there are alternatives.** It cannot be denied that **this gigantic propaganda drive** has had a considerable effect, especially on the young generation, and **has created a vast number of fanatics who will shrink from nothing** and who for this very reason are very formidable enemies.

16. Where We Stand

We mentioned already that German Nazism is the outcome of an enormous moral and social crisis in the midst of which we are living. The world is in the melting pot, and is being changed more rapidly and more drastically than ever before in the history of mankind. **Hitler and his satellites** claim that they are fighting for a new order, but in reality their so-called order is neither new nor is it, properly speaking, an order. They **stand** for something that is as old as the hills—**for tyranny**; they are trying to establish an Empire in which, as they quite cynically admit, **the German people will occupy the place in the sun,** and the others, **the inferior races, are going to be the drawers of water and the hewers of wood for the "Herrenvolk."** There is no doubt that we shall have to defeat their attempt to put the clock of history back by at least 500 years, but **we shall only defeat it permanently if we realise that we are fighting for a new order**, too; an order in which there is no question of a master race exploiting others, in which there is economic and political co-operation between the nations and in which freedom and human dignity are not trampled upon as they are in Germany, but are respected and safeguarded.

This new order is something worth fighting for, and we shall have the support of millions of people who to-day are groaning under the Nazi yoke all over Europe. And it is here that our conception of education comes in; **a better world can only be built by men and women who have learned to think for themselves**, who have an intelligent appreciation of the issues, and who have the necessary knowledge to tackle the numerous problems which will confront us.

The best army England ever had was Cromwell's, because his soldiers thought a lot and knew what they were fighting for. **The Nazis have turned their soldiers into ruthless robots; we shall defeat them with an army of free men who know they are fighting** not for narrow, selfish ends, but **for a better, cleaner and juster world. England** has taught the world the lesson of political freedom, it has shown mankind that an Empire can be based on justice and voluntary co-operation instead of on force. She **still has a magnificent mission, to rid the world of the ghastly disease of Nazism and to establish an order which will make its recurrence impossible.** It is our task to fill our men with a sense of that mission and to kindle in them **a spirit** of devotion which will be far stronger than the stupid and narrow fanaticism of the Nazi mind, because it is backed by the progressive forces in history.

Questions

Dr. Aris has frequently lectured on the Development of Nazism. These are some of the questions he has been asked and the answers that he has given.

(1) Q. *Are the German people behind Hitler?*
A. It is always difficult to generalise, but it seems that the majority of the Germans support the war even if many dislike the regime. The younger ones have been won over by skilful propaganda and many of the older ones have had some real benefits from the system, such as nice fat jobs. In Germany, as in all countries, the majority of people are indifferent and will support any regime as long as it is successful.

There are also many people in Germany who are afraid of the consequences of a defeat. They know some of the terrible things the Nazis have done in Poland, Jugoslavia, Russia and elsewhere, and they fear the vengeance of these peoples. We are, therefore, not fighting a small group of gangsters but the German people in its present mood, which is a desperate and dangerous one.

(2) Q. *Would Hitler's death make any difference to the war?*
A. It would be a severe blow to German morale, as Hitler has been built up into a myth and as many Germans firmly believe that he will not die until he has finished his task. On the other hand, it must be emphasised that the military conduct of the war is not in Hitler's hands, and if he died the generals would most certainly try to carry on.

(3) Q. *Is there dissension among the leaders of the Nazi Party?*
A. Yes. There always is in a dictatorial system, and gangsters usually quarrel amongst themselves, but none of the

sub-leaders has sufficient prestige to assume Hitler's rôle with the exception, perhaps, of Goering. In case of Hitler's death, however, there would most probably be serious trouble which would force the generals to take over political control.

(4) Q. *Why did Hitler attack Russia?*

A. He gave the answer himself in the speech which he delivered after the attack. He had realised that Great Britain could not be conquered by a blitzkrieg and he was afraid of exhausting his strength while Russia had time to complete her defences. If you read his book you will see that his primary aim was the conquest of Western Russia. Most probably he underestimated the military power of the Soviet Union; the generals certainly did, as is shown by their failure to supply winter equipment to the army fighting in Russia. When Hitler attacked Russia he was forced for the first time to give up his favourite strategy, which is to destroy one enemy after the other was finished.

(5) Q. *Why did Hitler assume responsibility for the military operations in Russia last winter?*

A. You know, perhaps, that Hitler is in any case the nominal C.-in-C. of all German Forces, but in reality military operations were carried out according to plans drawn up by the experts of the Army. It is pretty clear that the generals last winter objected to the last attack on Moscow, which proved such a spectacular failure. Hitler insisted on that attack not for military but for political reasons, and the generals in their turn demanded that the civilian should take full and open responsibility for an operation carried out against their advice.

The generals dislike to assume political responsibility themselves, and it is quite possible that they will leave

Hitler to his fate if it becomes clear that he is heading for catastrophe, just as in the last war they sacrificed their beloved emperor. They will try to survive this war as they survived the last one, but it will not be so easy to throw Hitler to the wolves as he and a small ring of men have set up an extremely powerful organisation in Germany. In the event of military defeat, however, this organisation will most probably break up, and it is then that we shall have to watch out. This time we must make sure that we destroy German militarism root and branch and do not allow the military leaders to get away with it again.

(6) Q. *Can Germany then carry on indefinitely?*
A. Certainly not, but as she has conquered the greater part of Europe she is strong enough to demand an absolutely supreme effort on the part of the United Nations. In spite of their large resources, the Nazi leaders have very serious worries, particularly as it becomes clear that this war is not a blitzkrieg. It would be foolish to make predictions, as we do not know enough about Germany's stocks, but it is quite clear that the transport problem, for instance, is one of the most serious ones, and you know that the R.A.F. is doing its very best to make it more serious still.

(7) Q. *Have the German casualties in Russia affected her man-power position?*
A. They certainly have had a very important effect. During the first two winters of the war Hitler sent many soldiers back into the factories to help in the production of war material. He could not do that last winter and he will not be able to do it in the coming winter. On the contrary, he had to comb the factories to replace his losses and the places of the called-up workers had to be taken by foreigners. Germany has reached the peak of its production, which is bound to

decline from now on, while the production of the United Nations is growing steadily from month to month. That the casualties in Russia must have been tremendous is shown by the frantic efforts of Dr. Goebbels to minimise them, and it is most characteristic that the Germans do not publish casualty lists. From obituary notices which appeared a few weeks ago in a leading Nazi paper it appears that men had been called back before they had completely recovered from former wounds.

WAR

The first time they saw Paris

ABCA 'War' Pamphlet No. 35, January 9th,
1943, pp. 11-13

- *German soldiers, by the author of "Death and To-morrow"*

The first time they saw Paris

by Pte. PETER de POLNAY, Pioneer Corps*

ON June 14th, 1940, early in the morning, I watched an endless grey stream moving down the Outer Boulevard. The German Army at the height of its good fortunes. Paris taken and the world more or less at its feet. They were young men those conquerors. Young and well disciplined. There was childlike wonder in their eyes. They were definitely surprised at having reached their goal so quickly and with such ease. After the many stories one heard of their cardboard tanks and bad equipment it was surprising to the onlookers how well equipped they were.

In a very short while they were all over Paris and because I speak German and belonged to (at that time) a neutral country I made many friends among them and found out quite a lot about them.

Too Old at Thirty-one

The troops that occupied Paris were crack troops. Young and fanatic they were. It was always the same story. The regular Army, the Spanish Civil War, the march into Austria and Czechoslovakia, Norway, Holland, Belgium and now France. They were trained for years and had their first innings in Spain. I remember speaking to a driver in the Panzers. He said that because he was 31 he was considered too old for active service: he drove a staff car. The

---

* Peter de Polnay was born in Budapest in 1906 and died in Paris in 1984. He had a long and successful writing career which included fiction and historical biography. His autobiography *My Road* was published in 1978.

morale of these men was excellent, but since they belonged to the elite of present-day Germany, and were professionals too, I don't attach too much importance to that. Anyway, most of them are dead by now.

They were conceited and flushed with victory. I must say, however, they respected the "Tommies." On the very day of occupation a soldier who alighted from a signals' car said to me: "We didn't take many British prisoners. They were usually dead or wounded." The man came straight from the battle of Calais.

Later the large mass of the conscript army lumbered into Paris. Many of their officers had taken part in the last war and they were, perhaps, more surprised at their easy victory than the youthful spearhead that had come before them. But the large majority of officers was young.

I knew of deserters. They were young men: the old didn't desert. Later in Vichy France I met two deserters. One had deserted because the life in France appealed to him more than German army life. He was 24. The other deserted because having hit a sergeant he was put into a punishment battalion. In that battalion discipline was so harsh that he couldn't stand more than four weeks of it. So he escaped into Vichy France and preferred the hell of a French prison to the soldiering he left behind. He was just 20 years old.

The Privates and the General

For discipline was harsh. But after duties there was very little of it. Officers and men mingled freely in the cafés and restaurants. A major in the infantry told me officers had special instructions to eat with their men in the Paris restaurants. None the less, each kept his distance, but officers never behaved like wet blankets. I often saw quite drunk soldiers being helped out of bars by officers.

I saw too in a small bar, where all the tables were occupied, two privates sitting down at a general's table. First, of course, they clicked heels and emitted lusty Heil Hitlers, then they sat down and ordered drinks. The general said a few words to them, then the soldiers drank and talked as though they weren't at the same table with the general.

When France fell Hitler promised that every German soldier of the battles of Flanders and France would see Paris. As far as I know that was the only promise Hitler ever kept. From all parts of France they came with their officers to partake of one day's tourist feast in Paris. I lived in Montmartre on the Place du Tertre, and usually the men, having finished with the nearby Sacre Cœur their sightseeing programme, were dismissed for an hour or so on the Place du Tertre.

They rushed into the bars and bistros and turned up at the rendezvous at least an hour late. The officers waited patiently and when at last the men appeared there hardly was a word of complaint. "You must have had a very good time," they mostly said. Rather surprising, for like many others I had heard a lot about Prussian discipline and the rest of it. I tried to find an explanation. I got one from a lieutenant-colonel. It sounded pretty convincing.

They Must Der Little Jokes Make

The lieutenant-colonel belonged to the Prussian officer class, his family for several generations had served Prussia and he, himself, had spent most of his life in the army. As he said, "I served the King of Prussia, the Weimar Republic and now Adolf Hitler. It is best to serve under him." Be that as it may, he said that the trouble in the last war was the collapse of the soldier's morale. In this war the General Staff wished to avoid the mistakes of the last war. So they concentrated on the relationship between officers and men and had reached the conclusion that it is far better to treat the men well and make them trust their officers as children trust their parents.

While on active service discipline is the most important factor in a soldier's life, but even so there are several opportunities to make the men feel happy. With German thoroughness they worked out a scheme, and German officers have definite instructions how to make the men feel happy in performing their duties. Heavy jokes at the right moment; expressing interest in their families; asking after their wives and children; and, I suppose, a few more heavy jokes. That, said the lieutenant-colonel, worked well. After duties complete freedom.

They found a compromise. In bars and even in night clubs the men salute their officers, but on the other hand they can go up to them, talk to them, joke with them, and, of course, when they leave they click heels and salute again. (Actually indoors they raise their arms and heil Hitler.) The officers must, after duties, treat their men as equals.

It Worked Remarkably Well

"Does it work?" I asked. He said it worked remarkably well. He went on to say that the fundamental principle of the Prussian military state had not changed. The Prussian Army's mainstay in the past was the landowner officer (Junker) and his tenants. A certain patriarchal system always existed in the Prussian (hence German) Army. Now it reached its modern conclusions. The officers were still drawn from the same class, only they had to treat their men in harmony with the new idea.

I inquired whether many men rose from the ranks. He said, very few. And if they did rise they went through the treadmill of the officer caste, and they either succeeded in achieving the standards of that caste or fell on the wayside.

More Than One Officer Led Away

In some matters they were very strict. Take, for instance, leave passes. After the first weeks of occupation the bulk of the German Army left Paris. The chief reason was that, having too good a time did discipline and morale a lot of harm. They were only allowed into Paris with special passes. That applied to officers and men. The German Military Police, the Feld Gendarmen, went the round of cafés and bars and asked for passes. They would stand to attention in front of officers, but inexorably ask for passes. I saw more than one officer led away by the Feld Gendarmen. The next move of officers and men alike was to buy civilian suits and try like that to evade the military police. There were notices on the walls of Paris that it was verboten to sell civilian suits to members of the Wehrmatcht [sic]. But there are always ways and means. The next move of the military police was to rope off in the evenings whole districts, post sentries everywhere and then methodically stop everybody in the district and examine the identity papers of all and sundry. As it isn't difficult to recognise a German their task wasn't difficult.

CURRENT AFFAIRS

Germany's New Order

ABCA 'Current Affairs' Pamphlet No. 41, April 10th, 1943

TALKING POINTS

THIS bulletin tells the story of how the Continent has been mobilised. It gives an account of Germany's design for Europe. What is the New Order? Does it apply to peace as well as to war? How was it imposed on Europe? Why was it accepted? What is its effect? Could the New Order bring peace to the Continent? What is the theory behind it all? If Europe remained a slave empire, how would this react on the rest of the world? These are some of the questions that Dr. Aris sets out to answer.

1. What is the New Order?

Germany's New Order is certainly a solution of all the problems of rival nationalities. Competition for raw material, competition for labour, competition for markets, all would be cut out. Europe would have the regularity of a machine instead of an organic life. It would be a machine for one purpose only. Only one nation could live and expand and develop itself, and that nation would be Germany. [IV.]

2. What Makes a Country or a Continent Accept Dictatorship?

It isn't only force. There are many motives that lead people to accept order, whatever that order may be. A strong motive is fear of disorder. Between the two wars nearly every country in Europe had experience of grave unemployment, if not of more serious trouble. Germany herself is an instance of the failure of a free government to solve these problems, causing the people to be prepared to surrender their freedom. This is but one of the things that make possible the rise of dictatorships. What are the others? [III.]

3. What is the Theory Behind it All?

Behind the German idea of World Domination there are two theories. One is economic (see 1 above), the other is racial. The Germans draw distinctions not only between German and foreign workers, but also among foreign workers themselves. And workers are paid according to their racial status. For instance, a Dane is higher "racially" than a Polish worker, and gets higher pay and more privileges. The racial order of foreign workers in Germany runs downwards roughly as follows:—

(a) Axis workers and workers coming from countries with which Germany has labour agreements—Italians, Spaniards, Hungarians, Bulgarians and Rumanians.

(b) "Nordic workers"—Netherlanders, Danes and Norwegians.

(c) Western European workers—French and Belgians.

(d) "Ostland workers"—Estonians, Latvians, Lithuanians and Czechs, Serbs and Croats.

(e) Poles and Russians.

And so the myth is worked out. The bayonet and the concentration camp have replaced the free labour market. Men, women and children are shifted about forcibly from one end of Europe to another. Millions of captives are exploited by a "master race" under an economic "blood hierarchy."

References for Further Reading
British Survey

Vol. 1, No. 6. Germany: Policy and Opinions, 1939.

Vol. 1, No. 7. Germany: Economic Conditions.

Vol. 2, No. 4. How a Nazi is Made.

Use the Keys

We call attention once more to the fact that the copious sub-headings in "Current Affairs" are not intended as typographical ornaments, but as the key to the material in the bulletin. By using those subheadings, a systematic talk and discussion can be ensured. They are the only notes an officer should need to take to the meeting if he has slowly and thoroughly digested the bulletin as a whole.

Germany's New Order

by Dr. R. ARIS

Dr. Aris is a full-time lecturer to H.M. Forces. He wrote the article in CURRENT AFFAIRS *No. 29, "The Development of Nazism."*

I. The Release of the Big Lie

1. No Warning in "Mein Kampf"

IF you read Hitler's book or the speeches of the Nazi bosses prior to the outbreak of the present war, you will look in vain for any mention of a New Order. This is not surprising when one remembers that it was Hitler's policy to deceive the peoples in the democracies and to make them believe that Nazism was not an article for export and would not interfere with the way of life of other nations. The Führer could not very well tell the world that he wanted to set up a New Order in which Germany was going to call the tune and the other countries were simply expected to dance to it. Had he done so the democracies might have taken notice and, forgetting their own troubles, have taken up arms and stopped the Nazi war-lords before the Panzer divisions and the squadrons of the Luftwaffe were ready.

2. Lies and Peace

All the speeches which the Führer poured out were therefore full of assurances of peace and goodwill towards all nations. Here is an example. It is to be found in a speech delivered on September 9th, 1936, at the opening of the Nuremberg Party rally: "The German people," so Hitler said, "has no other wish than to live in peace and friendship with all those who desire peace and who leave us undisturbed in our own country." If the world had only known Hitler in 1936 they would have realised that this statement simply meant: "My generals tell me that we are not quite ready yet for the 'Blitzkrieg,' so please leave us alone until we are." The world was taken in. It desired peace above all things and yet allowed the Nazis to build up the biggest war machine ever attempted. People simply refused to believe that anybody could be so mad as to want another world war barely twenty years after the last one. Governments hoped that the disaster could somehow be averted and that reason would prevail. It is easy to blame this or that politician now, but we should remember that most of us in those days ourselves believed in Hitler's assurances. The Englishman in particular is apt to forget injuries quickly and to help a beaten enemy on to his feet again. So Hitler went on pouring out glib assurances that he merely wanted to restore Germany's self-respect, that he had no evil designs on anybody except the Jews, and that a strong Germany was the surest bulwark against Bolshevism and the best guarantee for peace.

3. The Rape of Europe

Gradually, however, Hitler began to show his hand. In the first five years of his régime Germany had made considerable progress in her rearmament programme and the Führer felt that the stronger he became the more reluctant the democracies would be to risk a war. Austria was seized in March, 1938, despite Hitler's numerous declarations that "Germany neither intends nor wishes to interfere in the internal affairs of Austria" (Speech to the Reichstag, May 21st, 1935). The world was shaken when it learnt that an independent state had been wiped off the map in a few hours, but Hitler, the deed once done, was again full of assurances of goodwill towards other nations. In the autumn of the same year Czechoslovakia became his victim. A European war was only averted by a hair's breadth. But still, even after Munich, there were many people who believed that Hitler's ambitions were limited and that he merely wished to incorporate people of German race into the fatherland. It was Hitler's occupation of the whole of Czechoslovakia, although he had that same year declared that Germany did not want any Czech subjects, that undeceived these people. Finally, in 1939, when Poland was attacked, despite the treaty of friendship and non-aggression, Hitler's plans for world domination became clear.

4. Lies and War

Even after the outbreak of war, however, there was no sign of the so-called New Order. Even in war Hitler still hoped to carry on his policy of buying time with lies. He hoped to gain a few more years which he could use in digesting his spoils and perhaps in defeating Soviet Russia before he attacked the Western democracies. The New Order propaganda did not start in earnest until the summer of 1940 when Hitler realised that Britain would not give in and that the war would most probably be a long one. Quite suddenly and obviously according to a carefully worked out plan, the vast propaganda machine which Goebbels had set up began to pour out statements on the New Order. Germany no longer pretended that she was fighting for a modest place in the sun and that she merely wanted to liquidate the system of Versailles. She proclaimed that she was going to set up an entirely new order which would alter the political structure of Europe and would affect all the nations of the earth.

II. Promises Cost Nothing

1. As it was at Home

While the Nazis were fighting for power inside Germany before 1933 they employed a useful and simple device. They promised everything to everybody. As most of the population of Germany was dissatisfied, this worked very well. The farmers were promised a reduction in the cost of labour and high prices for food. The workers were promised high wages and cheap food. Before the eyes of industrialists were dangled the prospects of low wages and high profits. The shop-keepers were assured that the Nazis would destroy the big chain stores. It did not matter very much that some of these things could only be got at the expense of others. Many people swallowed the promises made to them and supported Hitler. In the end he was put into power by an intrigue and with the help of the industrialists and big business.

2. So it was to be Abroad

The Nazi leaders have always suffered from a curious delusion to which they still cling. It is to be seen again in the latest speeches of Goering and Goebbels. They think that what they had done inside Germany they can do in Europe and in the World. They forget that people outside Germany cannot be as easily hoodwinked as can Germans who have never really known what freedom means. They have completely overlooked the difference which exists between the weak and disunited democratic forces in Germany and the power and stamina of the great democracies. When Goebbels, therefore, started his New Order campaign in 1940, and when the Nazi hordes began to establish this order in those parts of Europe which Germany had conquered, they employed exactly the same strategy and methods which had been used so successfully in Germany.

3. Promises for All

All the occupied and Nazified radio stations of Europe poured out an interminable stream of promises. The Dutch were told that Germany would buy the produce of Dutch agriculture and market gardening. The Scandinavian states were assured that Germany would guard their economic interests and that they had better sever their trade connections with Great Britain, who was only interested in her Empire and had never shown any regard for Europe's prosperity. The Balkan states were promised a secure and stable market for their raw materials and foodstuffs, and financial help so that they could develop their resources. Even France was assured that she had a legitimate place in the New Order, provided of course that she did exactly what she was told and helped Germany to defeat that last obstacle on the path to victory, obstinate and unreasonable Britain.

4. Propaganda Succeeded at First

If you listened to all these cajoling voices in a dozen European languages you really began to wonder whether all this was not simply a gigantic joke and whether there could be anybody outside Germany who would take all this nonsense seriously. Was there anybody after all that had happened who would believe that Germany was fighting this war in the interests of all the nations she had trampled upon and robbed? Hypocritical as it was for the Nazi gangsters to pose as the magnanimous protectors of European unity, there is no doubt that this well-organised propaganda did not entirely fail. At any rate it did not fail during the first stage.

III. Idealists and Traitors

1. Wars had Prepared the Ground

Although Europe is the second smallest continent, it is perhaps the most important one of all. It is the cradle of Western civilisation and events that have taken place in it have influenced the fate of almost the whole world. On the other hand Europe is politically more disunited than any of the other continents. It is split up into a number of independent states which have waged war among themselves almost without a break. Several of these wars have engulfed large parts of the entire world. It is not surprising, therefore, that people should have dreamed of a united

Europe which would use its vast resources in the interests of all the European nations. Even if such far-reaching ideals as that of a United States of Europe were rejected as utopian and unpractical, many people thought that there should at least be economic unity. At a time when it takes an aeroplane only a few hours to fly from London to Warsaw, it seemed imperative that co-operation should replace the old policy of narrow-minded economic nationalism which had become antiquated and had proved disastrous to the prosperity of all nations.

2. Quislings and Collaborationists

All this must be borne in mind if we want to understand the chances which Nazi propaganda had of succeeding amongst the peoples of Europe. It must be remembered, too, that the years between the two wars had been years of trouble in Europe. There had been serious unemployment in almost every country and the constant threat of war had hung over Europe like a storm cloud. When the Nazis overran a great part of the continent in 1940 and 1941 there were quite a number of people who were at any rate willing to give the Germans a chance. They tried to believe that the Nazis were genuinely interested in European prosperity and not merely in their own bottomless pockets. Of course some of those people who collaborated with the Germans were just ordinary traitors, like Quisling*, who had been bribed and who hoped to feather their own nests by doing what their employers told them to do. Almost all the overrun countries produced a few such contemptible collaborationists. But on the whole the traitors were a small minority, useful and well paid for their treachery. Men who would never have achieved political prominence under

---

* Vidkun Quisling ran the Nazi puppet state in Norway during the war. His name subsequently became synonymous with 'traitor'. He was convicted on numerous charges by a Norwegian court and executed by firing squad in October 1945.

normal circumstances were given power. Men who had never been able to fill an honest job were given large salaries. It was from such material that Himmler selected the henchmen for his order of terror. It would be wrong, however, to think that all collaborationists were quislings. At first, at any rate, there were quite a few who honestly believed that the Germans would establish a new and better organised Europe. At the least they hoped that German domination would bring with it lasting peace. They knew that Germany would take the best of everything, but they tried to persuade themselves that there would be a modest share for them.

3. The Birth of Failure

Future historians will most probably ask themselves the question, "What was the turning point of Hitler's career?" There is little doubt that the answer will be that the Nazi system was doomed when Hitler failed to unite Europe behind him. If he had really succeeded in reorganising Europe and in winning the allegiance and loyalty of its inhabitants, the task of defeating him would have become immeasurably more difficult, if not impossible. Hitler not only failed to unite Europe behind him, he managed, on the contrary, to unite Europe as well as the greater part of the world against him in a titanic struggle in which the stake is no less than the future of civilisation. When Hitler failed to range the peoples of Europe behind him, his ultimate defeat was assured. Those people who had at first been deceived by the New Order propaganda soon came to realise that what the order really meant was slavery and economic misery for the vast majority of Europeans. They soon saw that Hitler was no more interested in the welfare of Europe than is the spider in the welfare of a fly caught in its web. How could Hitler be interested in the welfare of other nations when he had written in his book that nationalism means a fanatical belief in one's own nation and a supreme disregard for all others? How could he be expected to care for Norwegians, Czechs, Frenchmen, Greeks and Rumanians if he did not even care for the welfare of his own people, millions of whom he sacrificed to his insane ambition?

4. You Can't Fool All the People All the Time

It soon became quite clear that the much-advertised New Order was the most gigantic swindle ever invented. Hitler needed the man-power and resources of Europe to feed his insatiable war machine, and he hoped he could persuade the people of Europe to make all the sacrifices which the Germans themselves had made, by holding before them the same kind of vague promises which had been given to the German people.

In Germany he had succeeded. There he had found enough dupes to believe that all their terrific exertions and privations would bring about a period of glory and plenty for the German race. Outside Germany there was more scepticism and when it became apparent that the New Order was nothing but an extremely brutal and scientific form of exploitation and robbery, no amount of propaganda could disguise the fact.

IV. The New Order

1. How Simple was the Great Design

Everybody knows that some of the countries of Europe depend for their livelihood on their exports of manufactured goods. England and Belgium are countries of this kind. Others, like Denmark and Switzerland, are largely agricultural. Still others, like France and Germany itself, are industrial and agricultural producers at the same time. There has always been a great deal of competition between the industrial nations and the struggle for markets has often led to friction and wars between them. Nobody can deny that the problems which are inherent in this situation had not been solved after the last war and must be solved after this one if we want to establish peace and prosperity. Germany's New Order is nothing but an attempt to solve this problem in such a way as to benefit Germany and establish her economic security. But this way would in effect bring ruin to most other nations.

2. Ready Money was not Needed

Germany tried once before during the last war to establish her rule over Europe, and when her leaders thought the time had come for another attempt, she built up the largest war machine the world has ever seen. The plan for the execution of which Hitler had been appointed by the German industrialists was simple and ingenious. It was to build up a vast industrial machine which would ensure Germany's victory and then use that machine afterwards to conquer the markets of the world. That is the reason why the Germans never bothered about finishing their war effort properly. They hoped that other nations would in the end pay for it.

3. The Losers would Pay

For years Germany had been living on her capital and she devoted an ever increasing proportion of her national income to an enlargement of her industries for war purposes. Hitler boasted soon after the outbreak of the present war that more than 4,000 million pounds had been spent on armament, while the gigantic sacrifices which the German people had been induced to make in preparation for the war cannot be expressed in terms of money. The Nazi leaders knew that one day somebody would have to pay for all this. They knew that German industry would have to be switched back to peacetime production, and that unless it could sell its products huge unemployment would be the result. The Nazis therefore planned to organise Europe as a sort of arsenal for German industry and as a huge market for German goods.

4. There Would be no Rivals

Machinery in countries which might compete with Germany was going to be destroyed or to be transferred to the Reich. Rival industrial countries were to be reduced to the level of mere producers of food and raw materials. It did not interest these modern slave-drivers in the least that their policy of concentrating industry in Germany would seriously reduce the standard of living which had prevailed in the old industrial countries. The inhabitants of the exploited countries would have to put up with their rôle of hewers of wood and drawers of water for the master race or else to emigrate or commit suicide if they did not like it.

The French were told that they need not produce motor-cars in future. That would be done efficiently in the Reich. France should concentrate on growing vines and vegetables. The German propagandists made much of the French peasantry, a peasantry which, so the French were told, were the backbone of their beautiful civilisation. Of course the Germans did not themselves believe this nonsense. A nation which cannot build motor-cars cannot build tanks and aeroplanes. In consequence such a nation is pretty defenceless under modern conditions of warfare. By concentrating industry, especially heavy industry, in the Reich the Germans cunningly intended to ensure their own permanent superiority in armament, so that no nation could rise against their overlords, however sick they might have become of the New Order.

V. Sack of a Continent

1. The Robber State

The first thing the Nazis invariably did whenever they had conquered a country was to rob it of all its resources. The gold of the different state banks was transferred to the Reichsbank; stores of food, oil and wheat were confiscated. Valuable machines were removed to Germany and even art treasures taken away. It is well known that there has been looting in most wars, but it was left to the Nazis to turn looting into a fine art and to apply it on a gigantic scale and with scientific methods. The Nazis did not simply take away the food and raw materials of the conquered territories, they paid for them. Not in francs and guilders, of course, but in Reichmarks which had for a long time been completely valueless outside the Reich and which the inhabitants of the occupied territories were forced to accept at fantastic rates of exchange.

Apart from this "official" looting there were, of course, numerous cases of individual robbery carried out by German officers and men who took and sent home whatever they could lay their hands on. The result was that a few days after the German soldiers had arrived they cleared out all the shops so successfully that it looked as if the unfortunate country had been visited by a swarm of locusts.

2. Paying to be Robbed

On top of this the conquered territories were forced to pay vast sums for the maintenance of the German armies of occupation, and it is estimated that France alone has already been made to pay more than the Germans ever paid by way of reparations after the last war. This may be an exaggeration, but there is no doubt that Germany has extracted vast sums from her victims. In the case of France, for instance, the costs for the army of occupation were equivalent to what the French nation spent for the maintenance of an army more than ten times as big, and these costs were only slightly reduced when more than half of the forces of occupation were withdrawn. The Nazis also acquired enormous sums by confiscating all enemy property in Europe, although such procedure is forbidden by international law. The nominal value of British investments in Nazi-occupied Europe alone was placed at 250 million pounds and the property of the Polish State has been estimated at more than 600 million pounds.

3. Famine

Part of the money was used to buy shares in industrial and business concerns, and it is certainly no exaggeration to say that there is hardly an important firm in the whole of Nazi-occupied Europe which is not controlled by Germans. The Germans have thus acquired a stranglehold on the European economic system, by which they hope to maintain their war production. They expect to use this stranglehold in peacetime to ensure Germany's complete economic domination. The system of wholesale looting cleverly carried out under the cloak of strictly legal procedure has, of course, produced serious shortages of food and clothing in almost all the occupied countries, even in those which had formerly always produced a surplus. In some countries, Greece and France for instance, the result has been famine. The Nazis in vain tried to blame the British blockade for the terrible suffering in the occupied territories, the people knew quite well where their food went, and, if anybody still had any doubts, Goering made the situation quite clear when he said a few months ago: "If there has got to be a famine in Europe, it won't be in Germany." This one sentence completely exposed the hollowness of the New Order propaganda, and revealed to a horrified world the truth in all its brutality.

4. No Volunteers

In Nazi-controlled Europe people not only starve, they also have to slave for their masters, and thus help to perpetuate their own misery. Germany's war machine needs labour, and the greater the casualties in Russia become the more pressing becomes this need. At first the Nazis used promises and tried to persuade foreigners to come voluntarily into the Reich and work for Germany's war machine, but when the results of this campaign proved disappointing, force and blackmail were employed. Soon millions of workers were in German factories, living under military discipline in hastily built camps and drawing wages with which they could buy little. The alternative to this was starvation for themselves and their families, so they really had no choice.

5. Slavery

Sauckel,* who is the Nazi boss in charge of man-power problems, announced quite recently that there were about 7,000,000 foreigners working in Germany—truly slavery on a gigantic scale. It is true that these modern slaves work reluctantly for Germany, and there is a great deal of sabotage, but it cannot be overlooked that their labour helps Germany to some extent to solve its man-power problems, and it would be foolish to underrate the strength which Germany still derives from her brutal control of Europe's resources. On the other hand, the Nazi leaders are well aware of the danger which such a large number of foreigners on German soil presents. There is little doubt that one day these foreign workers will play their part in the destruction of a system which tries to enslave them permanently.

VI. The Theory Behind it All

1. A Superior Race

The Germans are known to be fond of theories, and even this fantastic and barbaric system of robbery and exploitation, which is Nazi Germany's special contribution to modern civilisation, is based on a theory. This is the theory of Germany's racial superiority with which Hitler filled pages of his notorious book. According to this theory, Germany is inhabited by a master race, superior in intelligence, industry, courage and organising power

---

* Fritz Sauckel was found guilty of war crimes at the Nuremberg trials and was hanged in October 1946.

to all the other races still living or extinct. Germany is, therefore, entitled to rule the world. Before the war Hitler merely claimed "Lebensraum" (living space) for the master race; after the fall of France he claimed that the German race alone would decide how much living space was to be allotted to the other "inferior" races.

2. What about Japs and Italians?

The Germans have even worked out a sort of racial scale which would be a thing to laugh at were it not for the appalling consequences which this madness has produced. At the bottom of this racial scale stand the Jews and the negroes; then, not very much higher up, come the Czechs and other Slavs; and on top are the blood-related races such as the Dutch and the Scandinavians, who are politely referred to as "auxiliary peoples." It is not exactly clear where the Italians come in on this scale, but there seems to be a growing suspicion among the Italians themselves that they do not come very high up. Nor is the racial position of the Japanese completely clear.

3. Lower Races Need Less Food

In their organisation of Europe the Nazis have applied this racial scale in practice. They are trying hard to exterminate the Jews, hundreds of thousands of whom have been murdered or starved or driven to suicide. The Slavs are not exterminated to the same extent. The Nazis need their man-power, so they are merely deprived of their intellectual leaders and denied facilities for higher education. "A lower race," so Dr. Ley said on January 31st, 1940, "needs less food, less clothes and less culture than a higher race." By killing the Polish teachers and professors, or by putting them into concentration camps, by shutting down secondary schools, the Nazis hope to make the Poles forget their national past so that they might become dumb and willing slaves of the master-race.

4. Contempt for the Common Man

In a way Germany's New Order is merely an extension to Europe of the system which they have set up inside the Reich. The Nazi State is based on the leader principle, according to which the mass of the people are expected to follow blindly and unquestioningly the commands of men who claim to be their born rulers. In his book Hitler has on several occasions expressed his contempt for the herd. That is why he expects his people to follow him like sheep, even if he leads them straight to the slaughter house. In the same way all the non-German races are expected to follow Germany's lead because Germany has a "mission" to organise and develop Europe. When the Nazis are amongst themselves, however, they give up all pretence and admit quite cynically that the chief purpose of the New Order is to benefit the German people at the expense of all others. "The peacetime economy," as Dr. Funk* said in his speech of July 25th, 1940, "must guarantee to Germany a maximum of economic security and to the German people a maximum consumption of goods. European economics must be directed to this end." In plain English, the Germans are going to get all that they want, while the others have to do all the dirty work and be content with what is left.

VII. Not Even the Peace of Death

1. The Odds are Not Even

The Nazi leaders have promised the peoples of Europe that their New Order would secure peace and would bring prosperity. In reality, of course, the New Order could only bring misery to the vast majority of Europeans. Nazi propagandists sometimes

---

* The economist Walther Funk was Reich Minister for Economic Affairs 1938–1945. He was tried for war crimes at Nuremberg and subsequently incarcerated in Spandau Prison until his release in 1957.

maintain that the misery which they have already brought to the conquered countries was not the result of German looting and exploitation, but was merely a temporary consequence of the war and would disappear as soon as Germany had won the war. But the bitter truth is that the ruthless and brutal imperialism of the New Order is bound to enslave and to impoverish its victims. Germany proposes to make Europe as self-supporting as possible so that it would become an impregnable fortress. That fortress, however, would be a prison for the 400 million Europeans who were not Germans and the prisoners would be perpetually condemned to living on short rations. Germany merely wants to play the old game of economic nationalism on a large scale. We ought to have learnt from the past that our economic problems can only be solved if all nations of the earth pool their resources and work together in the way proposed and visualised in the Atlantic Charter.

2. Customers are Not Right

It is true that the Germans will have to concede to the subjected races a certain minimum standard of living, as they need these people not only as working slaves, but as customers for their products. But as they propose to organise trade entirely in their own favour, and as the inferior partners of the New Order have no power to secure their own interests, their standard of life, particularly in countries where it was formerly high, as in France, Scandinavia and Holland, is bound to go down considerably. The Germans also hope, by controlling the whole of Europe and perhaps a great deal of Africa, to have such a strong bargaining position that they could force America and indeed the rest of the world to adjust their economic systems to the needs of the German Empire.

3. The Peace of the Grave

Before the war Hitler and Mussolini could not do enough to

extol the beauty and necessity of war, and one of the most important themes of Hitler's book is the glorification of war. Since the outbreak of this war, for which he is himself responsible, he has suddenly become a lover of peace and has again and again hypocritically asserted that he did not want war and that his victory would at last establish permanent peace. But the New Order would not even bring peace. It is true that the European nations, after having been deprived of their heavy industries, would not be able to make war to regain their freedom. But the peace "made in Germany" would be very much the same kind of peace which prevails in a concentration camp. People would live sullenly and without joy, as slaves did, and as many people living in Nazi-occupied Europe do at present.

4. Japan has a New Order, too

The New Order, moreover, is bound to clash with the rest of the world sooner or later, even if Hitler should succeed in overcoming his present opponents. In the Far East the Japanese, another "Herrenvolk," are trying to build up their version of the New Order on very similar lines. They want to exploit the vast resources of Asia and to use the gigantic reservoir of cheap labour which China could provide in order to flood the markets of the world with the products of sweated labour. Probably very soon German and Japanese imperialism would come to blows. The result would be another world war, perhaps even more gigantic than the present one. There is no hope of a lasting peace, no chance of happiness for any of us unless the Germans and the Japanese have been defeated and their plans to enslave the world have been thwarted.

VIII. Where do we Stand?

1. Could we Survive?

Great Britain, like other highly industrialised countries, depends for its livelihood on its ability to sell its coal and its manufactured goods in the markets of the world. If Germany won the war and established her New Order, or even if she merely succeeded in forcing a stalemate, she would be in a position to destroy the economic foundations on which our life is based. The markets in Europe would be completely closed to us, as the Germans would certainly not allow anybody to compete with German industry in this sphere. "We are going to do business solely on the basis of German advantage, and no American or British interests are going to put a stop to our way of doing business," so Hitler declared on February 24th, 1941, and on this occasion he certainly meant what he said.

2. The Competition of Slave Labour

The closing of markets in Europe would alone be a very serious matter, as Britain's trade with the Continent was quite considerable, but the Nazis would also be in a position to drive away competitors from the markets of the world. They could dictatorially regulate the wages and working conditions of the millions of slaves who work for them, and could, by a policy of subsidies and dumping, force the rest of the world to accept the conditions under which Germany was prepared to trade. The result would undoubtedly be that millions of people in Britain would be compelled either to starve or to emigrate. German propagandists have quite cynically visualised this consequence and have declared that there was plenty of room for millions of Britons in Canada or in the United States.

3. A War for Civilisation

"The two worlds are in conflict." So Hitler said on December 10th, 1940, and he continued, "One of these two worlds must break asunder." He was right on this point, even if in the same speech he gave expression to the belief that it would not be

Germany which would break. This is not a war for territories or tribute, as were so many wars of the past, when the vanquished lost a province or had to pay compensation and continued to exist very much in the same way as before. This is a war in which the whole future of our civilisation will be decided. It is a war whose outcome will affect every single one of us. We are fighting against a system which is based on brutal force, on the wicked and unchristian claim that there is one master race whose self-appointed leader can determine the fate of millions of civilised and freedom-loving human beings, a system by which the Nazi leaders seek to set up a rule of oppression and exploitation such as the world has never seen before and by which they want to put the clock back by at least five hundred years.

4. Where do we Stand?

It is not enough to know what we are fighting against; we must also know where we stand ourselves. The subjected races of Europe look to us not only for deliverance but also for guidance. We must tell them that we have taken arms not merely to destroy Germany's New Order but to set up a different order ourselves. The British Empire has shown the world that states can voluntarily co-operate on the basis of mutual respect and to mutual advantage, just as Britain has taught the world that efficient government can be combined with freedom and respect for human dignity. Nobody pretends that the world was perfect before Hitler plunged it into war, but we can claim that we are standing for progress, that we are at least trying to solve the difficult problems of our age in a spirit of tolerance and that we mean to establish freedom, without which life is meaningless. The peoples of Europe, and indeed of the world, must co-operate to solve the economic problems of our age, but that co-operation must be based on a genuine desire to give fair play to all and not on the insane ambition of a few men to set one race over all the others. Hitler's New Order would plunge the world into darkness and barbarism. That is precisely the reason why it is doomed to destruction and will be destroyed by forces which the Nazis have set into motion themselves, but which they have underrated and are unable to control. One day perhaps even the German people will learn the lesson that justice is more important than might. On that day the last trace of Hitler's New Order will have gone and it will be possible to build a better and juster world.

Questions

Dr. Aris has frequently lectured on Germany's New Order. These are short answers to some of the questions that he has been asked.

Q. Is Hitler succeeding in raising armies from occupied countries?
A. A few fanatics have joined the German Armies in Russia. Some of the contingents, like the Danish and Spanish ones, had to be sent back. It is unlikely that the Germans would dare to conscript men from the occupied territories for military service.

Q. Is there an anti-Nazi Party in Germany?
A. All organisations except the Nazi one are illegal. There is, however, an underground movement in Germany, and numerous threats against saboteurs are to be found in the speeches of all the Nazi leaders. The chief task of the S.S. is to guard the home front against the growing danger of riots and revolts.

Q. How does conscription of German women affect German morale?
A. It is fairly evident that the man-power position is Hitler's worst headache. About a year ago Sauckel was entrusted with the task of carrying out a total mobilisation of Germany's and Occupied Europe's man-power. The German leaders have had to carry out a short term policy of withdrawing skilled labour at the expense of future production, which is soon bound to suffer, even if we leave out of account the effects of R.A.F. raids. Neutral observers report that the Germans are beginning to feel the strain, and in a speech addressed to the women of Germany, a Nazi leader lately complained that too many women still shirked their duty. Now Goebbels, Goering and Sauckel have again ordered a still more complete mobilisation.

Q. Is it not true that slave labour is inefficient labour?

A. The Nazi leaders tried at first to lure foreign workers by all sorts of promises into Germany, but since the Russian campaigns the demand for man-power has become insatiable. The Nazis, therefore, increasingly had recourse to blackmail and threats, finally to wholesale conscription. The six million foreign slaves are an asset in Germany's economic balance sheet, but will one day turn into a dreadful liability.

Q. *Is there not the danger of complete chaos even in the occupied territories after our victory?*
A. The occupied territories will indeed need the help of the United Nations immediately an armistice is signed. The food situation in Europe is getting desperate. Disease and epidemics will have to be fought. The transport systems will have to be reorganised and many countries will need material help to make good depredations caused by "the new order." All these measures will require common action, out of which may grow a lasting reorganisation of this troubled continent.

CURRENT AFFAIRS

The Trouble With Germans

ABCA 'Current Affairs' Pamphlet No. 49, August 14th, 1943

TALKING POINTS

THIS pamphlet contains enough material for a serial ABCA discussion which could be initiated now, and again, at intervals till the end of the war. The pamphlet expresses one point of view about the Germans—and a pretty definite one, at that. There are other points of view on the subject; and no doubt your men will express them without much prodding on your part.

In dealing with this topic, you are not likely to be troubled by a shortage of men anxious to take part in the discussion; you are more likely to be troubled by the difficulty of trying to distinguish, and getting your men to distinguish, between fact and opinion.

Who Knows a German?

Bearing this in mind, it might be a good idea to encourage those members of your unit who have had some personal contact with some Germans to take part in the early stages of the discussion.

There may be, for instance, an old soldier who was billeted on an amiable German family during the 1919 Occupation; or a 21 year-old who saw refugees being machine-gunned on the Belgian roads in 1940, and who afterwards happened to be in the guardroom one day during the Battle of Britain when the crew of a German bomber were brought in.

Personal Experience or History?

If you find that two or more quite contrary opinions are expressed at the outset, you can then raise, in passing, the question of how far a man's view of the German nation in general may be coloured by his liking, or dislike, for some particular Germans he has known. How far is personal experience a valid basis for such generalised opinion? How far should it be corrected in the light of what appear to be historical facts? Says A: "I *know* the Germans. They're not as bad as that." Says B: "But look what they've done!" What are the clues to this "contradiction"? There are people who say that the answer lies in the misleading use of the lump-term "the Germans." Germany, these people argue, breeds bad Germans and good Germans. On the other hand, there are a great number of other people who, like the writer of this pamphlet, say in effect—and on this point you can steer the discussion out of its preliminary stage—that:

"The Germans don't Change"

Is this so? Is Hitler the contemporary embodiment of the unchanging German lust for domination? Are Nazis representative Germans? Is Nazidom simply the 1930-40 vintage of the native German liquor which has been brewed for centuries past? (See "Current Affairs," Number 9—"Know your Enemy"; also Number 41—"Germany's New Order.")

Were the Kaiser's armies intoxicated with the same sort of fanaticism, and as much of it, in the last war, as Hitler's armies have been in this war? Has the mental attitude of the Nazi soldier who invaded Poland in 1939 more in common with the mental attitude of the Imperial German soldier who invaded Belgium in 1914, than he has with Mussolini's Fascist legionary who invaded Abyssinia in 1935?

Are Nazi troops just the way they are (a) because of some national characteristic? Or (b) because of some political creed and philosophy which is not confined to one nation? Or (c) because of a combination of both things?

"... And They Yearn to be Led"

If it's a fact that the Germans don't change, is there a biological reason why the men of a certain nation should always be born more aggressive than the men of other nations?

Or is the answer, as the writer of this pamphlet says, that the Germans follow their leader, and for over 100 years their Leaders have been aggressive?

In that case, would there be more hope for ultimate peace in Europe if, eventually, some German leaders were discovered who were not aggressive? Would that fix everything?

In any case, the Germans are far from being beaten yet. And that can bring you to the next stage in the discussion:—Just how far are the Germans from being beaten? What, in fact, is the state of

German Morale To-day?

The writer of the pamphlet points out that the morale of the German armed forces on the continent is still unshaken. Indeed, it is well to remember that, until we are actually inside Berlin, there may always be some temptation to wishful thinking on the subject of enemy morale.

For Instance: do your men feel inclined to believe the occasional reports that German troops in Norway are beginning to desert across the Swedish frontier, or that U-boat crews are beginning to feel that the sea is not all that it's cracked up to be?

Would such reports be important if they were true? What caused the mutiny of German sailors at Kiel, which appeared to hasten the German collapse in the last weeks of the First Great War?

The morale of German civilians to-day? Here again it is important, as well as difficult, to try and distinguish between fact and opinion. What, for instance, do your men think of the story of the "revolt of the Munich students"?*

What Affects Enemy Morale?

How can the morale of the German armed forces and the civil population's will to resist be weakened by the United Nations? Are there any other means besides military action?

---

* It was recently reported that the Students Union of Munich University had been involved in an anti-Nazi movement, whose aim was to establish "true science and spiritual freedom" in Germany; that six of the leading students had been caught by the Gestapo and hanged; and that others had been imprisoned.

How was the will to resist of the Italian army and people weakened? By the invasion of Sicily and the Allied bombing, only? Or by that plus the Churchill-Roosevelt messages to the Italian people?

The writer of this pamphlet implies that the fear of alternatives—the fear of what the Allies will do to Germany if they win—plays its part in strengthening the German will to resist. Could their will to resist be weakened if the Allies removed the fear? Would it be desirable to do this, or not?

Would the public promise of what Sir Paul Dukes calls "a surgical operation" (see section 12) weaken the German will to resist? A surgical operation, incidentally, performed by whom on exactly whom? By some Germans on other Germans? Or by British, Americans, Russians and the rest of the United Nations on all Germans? Or what?

What, in your opinion, are the most useful sort of things that we could broadcast to those Germans who risk their lives listening to the British Radio?

Can Germany be De-contaminated?

Finally, is a nation like the twentieth century German nation capable not only of adopting formal democratic institutions, but also of becoming democratic in spirit and attitude?

By what steps could democratic institutions be recreated? By what means could the minds of young Nazis be de-contaminated?

What helpful part could German women—some of whom are now reported in the neutral press to be already war-weary—be expected to play in any future transformation of their country? Of what future value to Germany and Europe are likely to be those thousands of Germans who have been imprisoned by the Gestapo because they were considered to be dangerous to the Nazis?

What elements, if any, of a constructive opposition to Hitlerism and power-striving German Imperialism are there inside Germany to-day? If they exist, is there any use that can be made of them?

QUIZ

1. What's the difference between the S.A. and the S.S.? [Section 1]

2. Do the S.S. go into action? What are their other functions? [1]

3. What German State took the lead in uniting Germany? [4]

4. Was Hitler's Master Race idea an original one? Or had any Germans thought it up before? [5]

5. Besides the Kaiser, were there any kings about in Germany in 1918? [3]

6. What was Hitler's "Strength-through-Joy" movement? [11]

7. What has replaced the Trade Unions in Germany? [11]

8. What does a German woman have to do before she can be accepted by the Nazis as having attained full citizenship? [10]

9. Was the Armistice of 1918 "conditional" or "unconditional"? [12]

10. What does Hitler's "New Order" amount to? [6]

11. What is the Nazi leaders' doctrine about Christianity? [7]

The Trouble With Germans

by Sir PAUL DUKES, K.B.E.

German Morale To-day

1. How is it in the Fighting Forces?

IN spite of the reverses suffered by the Axis during the past winter it would be a mistake to underestimate German morale. Indications are that, on the Continent, it is still unshaken. Though German air activity is obviously suffering from forced restrictions, there are no signs of weakening morale in the Luftwaffe; and, in sea warfare, U-boat crews continue to go blindly to their task. Cases of unreliability, if any, are more likely to be found in the army, but they still appear to be rare.

Where do the S.A. Come In?

What is the explanation? Firstly, the composition of the German army is quite unlike that of our own army. In addition to the Wehrmacht, or regular army, there are "S.A." (Sturm-Abteilungen), or Storm Troops (sometimes called Brown Shirts), and "S.S." (Schutz-Staffel), a special organisation, half police, half military in character, sometimes called Black Guards. The S.A. constituted Hitler's private army when he came to power, and have retained their organisation ever since. The S.S. are carefully selected units, picked for their physique and proven political fanaticism.

Storm Troops (S.A.) are allocated to all military units in the proportion of about 10 per cent. The S.S. are a more privileged organisation, reserved for special functions. The Fighting S.S. Divisions correspond in a sense to our Guards, but the S.S. are also given the task, in conjunction with the Gestapo, of controlling the civilian population both within Germany and in occupied territories. This composition of the German army makes its texture very strong.

The Best of Everything

All branches of the forces are highly disciplined, and constantly subjected to intensive propaganda which transforms them into unthinking fighting robots. They are treated to the best available food and outfit. Consequently, though an over-rigid structure such as that of the Nazi State is likely to collapse suddenly and completely when it does begin to crack, we should nevertheless guard against imagining that, on the Continent, anything like the cracking point has yet been reached.

2. What about the Civilians?

Who constitute the civilian population of Germany to-day? Apart from the ruling Nazi bureaucracy, the civilian population consists largely of (a) elderly people who no longer count; (b) the women, the majority of whom are engaged in conscripted war work; (c) the male workers, who are being supplemented in ever-increasing numbers by conscripted workers from the occupied territories; and (c) children. Undoubtedly among the adults, especially the elderly who remember saner times, there are elements opposed to Nazi philosophy; high Church dignitaries, for instance, have repeatedly protested against Nazi doctrines. But they are unarmed, and they could not organise revolt, even if they wished to. Besides—and this is a vital point to remember—unlike the Briton, who likes to hold and express an opinion of his own, the German, in things political, is by nature obedient and submissive. The German worships "authority," and the more strict and even brutal that "authority" the more he seems to respect it.

What Alternatives Have the Germans?

Hitler represents "authority" in a more intense and concentrated form than the German people have ever before known. To reinforce this authority Hitler aims to fill the Germans with fear of the alternatives. Official propaganda spares no efforts to depict the horrors that must befall the German people if Germany loses the war. Consequently, though military reverses may make the people despondent, they will also make them clench their teeth. As with the army, the break-up is likely to come suddenly, as it did in 1918, and some unpredictable factor is likely to cause the crack.

The German Mould

3. Are Germans More Easily Led than Other People?

They are certainly much more easily led than ourselves. The reason for this lies in the difference between British and German history. The English, Welsh and Scots, despite different national characteristics and customs, learnt long ago to regard themselves as one community, one family, one nation, under one Head and with one Parliament. This unification of national sentiment was facilitated by our island position.

German "Unity" Came Late

German history, like her geography, is in marked contrast—and geography always plays a large part in determining history. In Germany, the national unification which we have so long enjoyed has only just come about. Indeed, Hitler is the first German ruler ever completely to achieve it. Long after Great Britain had become a unified political entity Germany was still a loose agglomeration of separate states with separate rulers (at the beginning of the 19th century there were still over 300 of them!), and they were often at war. The Napoleonic wars resulted in a reduction of the number of states, and Bismarck made a great step towards unifying the remainder in 1871, but even then several of the individual rulers retained their thrones.

When Germany collapsed in 1918 not only the Kaiser, but with him over 20 German kings and potentates lost their crowns. The Kaiser had been, as one might say, president of the German kings, a sort of royal chairman of a board of crowned directors, but he was not all-powerful though he liked to call himself so.

"To Submit, to Follow ..."

The course of German history has thus been very different from British. When the British people achieved their unification they settled down to evolve that high degree of liberty and self-government which we now enjoy. But this took time, and the Germans have not had the time, even if they had the will, to do this. The foundation of our liberties was laid many centuries ago with Magna Carta. The Germans have never had a Magna Carta; it is not in their nature to demand one and they wouldn't know what to do with it. The Germans have produced great artists, scientists, musicians, and philosophers, but their works were the product of individual, not of community, genius. The British system of self-government was created by no one man; it is a development of community genius.

The German's dream has not been of liberty or self-government so much as of unification under some central head. In this longing lay the germs of the Führerprinzip. The Germans have yearned for a Führer, a Leader, who would unite them, and submission to such a leader is deemed by them the highest virtue. This is the reason why, in politics, the Germans are easily led—because their history has made them desire to be led. Nietzsche wrote of this quality: "To submit, to follow, this is a German virtue; to achieve obedience to a person is the cult of the German."

The Blood and Iron Tradition

4. Why are the German People Aggressive?

They are aggressive because for over 100 years their leaders have been aggressive, and they follow the leader.

The aggressive spirit has been sedulously cultivated in Prussia, the largest German state, since the time of Frederick the Great, who died in 1786. Prussia has always taken the lead in movements for unification of the German states and their expansion into an Empire. By aggressive wars throughout the 19th century Prussia expanded her own borders to embrace many of the smaller north German states. She subdued her rival Austria, then conquered France, and under Bismarck formed the first German Reich in 1871. All the states except Austria entered this Union under Prussian leadership, though they retained separate rulers and parliaments. From that time onward the Prussian spirit permeated the whole of territorial Germany. Aggression and war enabled Prussia to achieve her dominating position, so aggression and war became the national philosophy, and the Germans, led by this spirit, came easily to believe that might was right.

"Neither Law nor Right Exists ..."

Already before Napoleon's time the Prussian philosopher Fichte, who strongly influenced German thought, wrote: "In his (the King's) relations with other states neither law nor right exists except the right of the strongest." And the greatest of all German political philosophers, Von Treitschke, wrote in 1869: "Martial force is the basis of all political virtues. ... That war should ever be banished from the world is a hope not only absurd but profoundly immoral. It would involve the atrophy of many of the essential and sublime forces of the human soul and transform the globe into a vast temple of egoism." Thus encouraged, it was no wonder the Germans became intoxicated with dreams of unbounded conquest.

The Superman Myth

5. Why do the Germans Claim to be the "Herrenvolk"?

The Germans apply this term, meaning "master race" or "overlord people," to themselves on the ground that they are racially—that is, biologically—superior to all other peoples. The British are a mixed race—a mongrel breed of Teutons, Latins, Celts and many others—and are therefore regarded as "inferior." The Germans, by contrast, claim that they are the thoroughbreds, unpolluted by mongrel infection. They are "the master race" that has "dominated central Europe since the beginning of time."

This claim is made arbitrarily and has been one of the favourite themes of German political philosophy. The highest race among humankind is said to be the Aryan, and among Aryans German blood is claimed to be the purest. The Germans are therefore the salt of the earth, the supreme development of civilisation. Germans therefore have a natural right to rule others.

"Deutschland, Deutschland" is not New

It is not difficult to trace this doctrine to an overwhelming inferiority complex, which finds its most tortured and hysterical expression in Adolf Hitler. But it is very important for an understanding of the German problem as a whole to remember that the doctrine is not Hitler's invention. It has been preached for a long time to justify Germany's right of aggression. The Germans have been taught that by undertaking a new war every few decades with a view to expanding the sphere of German domination they are fulfilling a sacred mission, the spreading of German *Kultur*. The hymn *Deutschland, Deutschland über alles, über alles in der Welt* ("Germany, Germany over everyone, over everyone in the world") is not a new hymn. It was the German national anthem in the last Great War. The Germans, politically backward and easily flattered, have taken the doctrine of their biological superiority quite seriously.

Those Inferior Peoples

Note the dates of the following quotations. A pamphlet by the All-German League in 1891 said: "We must raise higher the banner of Pan-Germanism. ... The nation must know *why* for decades to come they will have to prepare with increasing exertion to arm themselves and fight." In 1901 an anonymous pamphlet was published advocating a German World-State, which contained the following (quoted in *Thus Spake Germany*, edited by W. W. Coole and M. F. Potter): "Germans alone will govern; they alone will exercise political rights; they alone will serve in the army and navy; they alone will have the right to become landowners. ... However, they will condescend so far as to delegate inferior tasks to foreign subjects subservient to Germany." Professor Joseph Reimer, a well-known political writer, wrote in *Principles of German Revival*, in 1905: "Our race with its culture is superior to all other nations and races of the earth ... Our civilisation has reached a height where it incomparably excels and dominates that of all the nations of the earth."

Shakespeare was O.K.

German theorists go to remarkable lengths in their efforts to show that everything worth while that has ever been done in the world was done only by men of German race. Thus the philosophical writer Julius Langbehn wrote in his *Rembrandt as Educator*, in 1890: "The German who recognises Shakespeare and Rembrandt as men of the same blood as himself recognises Cromwell and Pitt as the same also; and the time will certainly come when the Dutch, the English, the Danes, the Swedes will salute their spiritual forbears not only in Luther, but in Bismarck."

Was Hitler so Original?

It is important to remember that all this was written long ago, and that these doctrines are typically German and not merely Hitlerian. After the last Great War we foolishly allowed them to be revived and become concentrated in the person of Hitler. But the horrors perpetrated in Europe to-day, the allocation of inferior rôles to "inferior" peoples, the subordination of the whole continent, are a fixed German policy which will be revived again even after the defeat of Hitler, unless more effective measures are taken by us than were taken after 1918.

Hitler's Contributions

6. What is this "New Order" of Hitler's?

Reduced to its simplest terms, it is a plan for the reorganisation of Europe in two main divisions: (a) an expanded Germany which shall include all the chief industrial areas of Central Europe, and (b) an agricultural remainder consisting mainly of France, the Balkans, Poland, and parts of Russia, which shall feed the industrial centre. (Italy is not officially provided for, but would presumably reap the benefits of German partnership.) It is claimed that economic stability would be achieved by the exchange of Germany's finished articles for raw materials and food; a market for surpluses would be assured to associated states; and peace in Europe would be secured through the whole of the Continent becoming virtually a German protectorate.

A Paying Proposition

In this scheme of things satellite states would retain their nominal political independence and develop along traditional cultural lines; but the whole of their economy, their industries, communications, and banking systems, would be linked up and co-ordinated in

Berlin. There would be a double currency; the German mark would be accepted throughout Europe, while for local purposes local currencies, pegged to the mark, would continue to circulate. The size of national defence forces would also be controlled by Germany, who would arbitrate in all disputes. Propagandists argue that the harnessing to Germany's driving power of non-German labour, with unified distribution of commodities, would have incalculable benefits and raise the general standard of living—indeed, that it would be in the German interest to improve the standard of living of satellite peoples in order to raise their standard of production. Moreover, Germany as the controlling instance would acquire a monopoly of extra-European markets and therefore huge bargaining power with the rest of the world.

"A Lower Race Needs Less Food ..."

Such a system might find some justification if the superior wisdom and right of domination of the Herrenvolk were conceded. But that the welfare of the subsidiary states would in practice be a very secondary consideration was frankly admitted by Dr. Funk, Minister of Economics, in a speech on the New Order on September 1st, 1940, in which he said: "The peacetime economy of Europe must guarantee *to the German Reich* a maximum of security and *to the German people* a maximum consumption of goods to increase their welfare; all European economics must be directed to this end." While on January 31st, 1940, he laid down the principle that "a lower race needs less food, less clothes, and less culture than a higher race." In Occupied Poland to-day a German gets nearly twice as much food as those Poles who are working under compulsion for the Germans.

The picture is clear: Germany is not interested in the real welfare of the European states, but only in her own, to which all other countries must minister, while the New Order would be administered by the Hitler Youth grown to maturity and impregnated with contempt for the satellite peoples.

Hitler's Children

7. What is the "Hitler Youth"?

It is an organisation which all school children must join, graduating from it into the semi-military organisations of the Labour Service. Its object is to supplant parental influence, secure control of the adolescent mind, and train the youth of Germany to be blind devotees of Hitler. In his speech of May 1st, 1937, Hitler said, referring to parental opposition to this system: "We will take the children away and train and educate them to become new Germans ... We will take them away when they are 10 years old and bring them up in the spirit of the community until they are 18. They shall not escape us. They will join the Party, the Storm Troopers, the Black Guards or other formations, or go into the factories and offices. Later on they will do military service. Who shall dare say that such training will not produce a new nation?"

All Nazi schooling is designed to produce a generation of soldiers and young mothers ignorant of conditions outside Germany and with grotesque ideas about the rest of the world, but fanatically believing in Hitler as the God-sent saviour whom it is their privilege to serve. On Hitler's access to power the teaching profession was combed out, and the first qualification for admission to its ranks became the possession of a Party ticket. The resultant shortage of teachers was never quite made good, even with an influx of inferior teachers; but the Nazis did not bother about this, they merely curtailed the schooling period.

Education for Death

The complete mental Nazification of the growing generation is a factor with which we shall have to reckon long after Hitler is overthrown. Every school subject is taught first and foremost from a political standpoint with a political object. A vast number of scientific works was proscribed in 1933 as being contrary to the new doctrines, and the writings of learned Jewish authors were publicly burnt. In their place new textbooks have been issued which present everything—history, literature, even mathematics and science—from a racial standpoint, designed to glorify Germany and train the children to become unthinking followers of Hitler in the coming conquest of the world. Two songs are always sung, not merely as patriotic ditties, but as a profession of faith: *Deutschland über alles*, and another, the last line of which is *Heute gehört uns Deutschland undermorgen die ganze Welt* ("The world will be ours to-morrow as Germany is to-day").

Any attempt on the part of parents to inculcate any other principles, such as Christian teachings for the home, is vigorously condemned. The children are ordered to report to the authorities if their parents make the slightest criticism of the official doctrine, so that an atmosphere of fear, suspicion and mutual distrust often grows up even in families where formerly the greatest affection prevailed. From the moment when nobody dares speak the family, of course, becomes senseless. Parents are ordered to answer, when asked by their children "To whom do we really belong?" only "You belong to the Führer."

Christianity with a Difference

The credo at school runs as follows: "Adolf Hitler, to thee alone we are bound. In this hour we renew our solemn vow; we believe in this world in Adolf Hitler alone. We believe that National Socialism is the sole faith to make our people blessed. We believe there is a Lord God in heaven who has made us, who leads us, who guides us and visibly blesses us. We believe the Lord God has sent Adolf Hitler that Germany should be established for all eternity." Alfred Rosenberg, a leading Nazi theorist, wrote in *The Mythus of the 20th Century* (p. 623): "All German education must be based on recognition of the fact that it is not Christianity that has brought us morality, but Christianity that owes its enduring values to the German character."

To sum up. Nazi education is designed to turn the male youth into fanatical warriors, and the female youth into no less fanatical mothers of a further generation of fanatical warriors. But, looking back once again, we find that this also is not new. The same spirit was fanned in the German youth long ago. In 1909, Thomas Kaemmerer wrote in an article entitled 'The Coming World War,' in the magazine *Hochaktuel* : "Probably in no country is war so popular as in Germany, and the older generation, who regard war as the arena of glory and honour, are seeing to it that it remains so. German youth dreams only of war, plays only the game of war."

Hitler's Deity

8. What Sort of God Does Hitler Believe In?

If Hitler really believes in the Almighty it is certainly only on the assumption that God is a German. But in this also he is not original. The Kaiser did the same, speaking of "Unser deutscher Gott" (Our German God). In 1914 his proclamation to the German armies at the commencement of hostilities ran thus: "Germans, remember you are the chosen people. The spirit of the Lord has descended upon me, because I am the Emperor of the Germans. I am the instrument of the Most High. I am His sword, His representative. Woe and death to those who do not believe in my mission; Let them perish—all the enemies of the German people: God demands their destruction—God who through my lips commands you to execute His will."

Protesting Against What?

Hitler merely carries on a German tradition. Neither the Kaiser nor Hitler would have any use for a God who regarded other peoples on an equal footing with Germans. This feeling is deep-rooted in Germany. It is true that several prelates have protested against Hitler's attitude to the Church and the restrictions placed on

Church practices and customs; they have protested against the persecution of the Jews, against mass-executions and the doing-away with alleged mental defectives in lethal chambers; but they have protested against these horrors only as incidents, they have not protested against Hitler's ever having launched this war. They have not yet denied Germany's right of aggression, and the evidence is that most of them would still prefer to see a German victory.

Make Room for the Germans!

9. What is the Doctrine of "Lebensraum"?

"Lebensraum" means "living space," and the theory of how much elbow room or living space the Germans should have in the world is intimately bound up with the theory of the New Order.

Volumes have been written by German theorists on this subject. The definition of Lebensraum may vary according to whether the matter is approached from a historical, racial, cultural, linguistic, economic or political angle, but in a nutshell it may be summed up thus: the Master People, creating a New Order in the world, have the right to determine for themselves how much "elbow room" they need, or in other words, where their State boundaries are to be. Robert Sieger (quoted in *The German Lebensraum*, by R. E. Dickenson, p. 20) puts it thus: "Boundaries will be felt as organic boundaries if they do not cramp the State and its people, but allow unhampered development of the political functions *and fulfilment of the State's purpose.*" The State's purpose in the present case being the establishment of the New Order, the boundaries of Germany are to be established as best suits that purpose.

Anvils or Hammers?

This doctrine also is not new. Friedrich Ratzel, professor of geography at Munich and Leipzig, wrote in 1905 in his *Naval and World Questions*: "There will always be master-peoples and slave-peoples. The peoples themselves have only the choice between being anvils and hammers ..."

Professor Ludwig Reimer in *Principles of German Revival*, in 1905: ... "We must: (a) Germanize the Scandinavian states and the Low Countries (b) disintegrate the non-German peoples ... to make them German and expel that which is non-German in them. Thus we shall return to the primitive German race while conquering new territories; we shall have a vaster land and a purer race."

These wild hopes, expressed before the last Great War and dashed by it to the ground, have now been revived with renewed force. Hitler did not invent them, he merely utters them with a greater fanaticism. It was always the aggressive Prussian spirit which inspired him, as he admits on page 527 of *Mein Kampf*: "The organisation of the Prussian State, which was the work of the Hohenzollerns, became the model for the crystallisation of a new Reich."

Hitler and the Gentle Sex

10. What is the Position of Women in Germany?

Hitler has made his views on women quite clear in *Mein Kampf*, p. 459: "In the case of female education the main stress should be laid on bodily training, after that on development of character, and only last of all on the intellect. The one absolute aim of female education must be towards future motherhood." Thus women in the Nazi state are regarded primarily as breeders. They are not expected to take part in politics. A woman does not acquire full citizenship until she has borne a child. She is encouraged to marry early, and children born out of wedlock are regarded as on the same footing as those born in wedlock, provided the parents are pure German. Inter-racial marriages are forbidden.

"Whether or not she is Married"

The childless woman of 25 or over is regarded as a shame and a burden to the State—she has not fulfilled her function. Alfred Rosenberg, in *The Mythus of the 20th Century*, expresses it thus: "The German Reich of the future will have to regard the childless woman, regardless of whether or not she is married, as an incomplete member of the national commonwealth." Women who are not about to bear children or who have no children to look after, either because they are childless or because they have handed over their children to the care of the State, work in factories or on the land. But the prime function of woman in the Nazi State is to produce the maximum number of children by fathers of pure German blood.

"Monogamy is Perverse ..."

In this view of the subject love and fidelity in marriage become of secondary importance. It does not matter much who the parents are as long as they are of German blood. Ernst Bergmann, professor of philosophy at Leipzig, in an essay on *Knowledge and the Spirit of Motherhood*, expressed the matter thus: "Life-long monogamy is perverse and would prove harmful to our race. Were this institution ever really enforced—fortunately this is never the case in reality—the race must decay. Every reasonably constructed state will have to regard a woman who has not given birth as dishonoured. There are plenty of willing and qualified youths ready to unite with the girls and women on hand. Fortunately one boy of good race suffices for 20 girls. And the girls for their part would gladly fulfil the demand for children were it not for the nonsensical so-called civilised idea of the monogamous permanent marriage, an idea in complete contradiction to all natural facts." (Quoted by E. Mann in *School for Barbarians*, a study of education under the Nazis.)

Hitler and the German Workers

11. What is Hitler's Attitude Towards Labour?

Before coming to power Hitler boasted of the benefits he was going to confer on the workers, whose special advocate he proclaimed himself to be. Indeed, the full title of the Nazi Party is the "National Socialist German Workers' Party." By eliminating unemployment through expansion of armaments, and by certain housing and other reforms, he did succeed in getting the support of the workers. But whatever he gave with one hand was more than taken away with the other, and the last state of the workers is definitely worse than the first.

"Suppression, Arrests, Confiscation ..."

There were seven million unemployed when Hitler came to power; when he invaded Poland in 1939 there was not only a shortage of labour, but labour was being imported from abroad. The change was brought about by spending vast sums, not only on armaments, but on public works, repairs to farms, housing schemes, and the construction of military roads. But while these visible developments were taking place (to the admiration of some foreign observers who did not look behind the scenes) the workers were rapidly being deprived of the last vestiges of the rights and liberties they had enjoyed under the Weimar republic. In the first year of the Hitler regime all trade unions were suppressed, union leaders arrested and union property confiscated. The social-democratic party was declared illegal, and the formation of any new party forbidden.

What Happened to the Trade Unions?

The Führerprinzip was introduced into industry, proprietors of undertakings being made little führers. The factory-führer was to be advised by confidential councils elected by the workers, but in

1935 these councils ceased to be elective, and were nominated by "labour trustees," officials appointed by the Ministry of Labour to supervise large economic areas. Labour conscription, and all those restrictions which in Britain have been voluntarily accepted as a wartime necessity, were introduced in Germany by the Nazis as normal peacetime legislation. But whereas in Britain the union organisations remain intact, playing a part in the government and a more important role than ever before, in Germany these measures were forced on the workers by decrees of a single-party government which had abolished trade unions altogether.

"Strength-Through-What?"

In place of trade unions an institution known as the Labour Front was set up, consisting of both employers and employed. It is a sort of guild on a national scale, but directed by the National Socialist Party. Its funds are derived from compulsory levies on its members. No account is rendered of these funds, so that the Labour Front becomes in practice an instrument for the collection of additional taxation both from employers and workers. It also supplements the Gestapo by reporting any signs of discontent. The Labour Front has no jurisdiction in regard to wages, hours, or conditions of employment, which are in the hands of the Ministry of Labour. But an attempt is made to offset the loss of liberty by other functions of the Labour Front, which administers relief, amenities in factories, general welfare, and the much-vaunted "Strength-through-Joy" movement, which provides millions of workers with cheap holidays and excursions, entertainments, athletics, concerts and so forth.

More Housing Space than Poles or Jews

Though German workers have shown some independence in the past, it would be a mistake to suppose that they are exempt from the common German proclivity to submit and obey. They have fallen into the traps laid for them, through the inherent tendency to follow the Leader. Consequently, it is not surprising to hear the head of the Labour Front, Dr. Ley, exhorting the German workers in the following terms (*Deutsche Allgemeine Zeitung*, November 10th, 1940): "The higher a nation stands racially the greater must be its requirements. The German needs more housing space and a better standard of life than the Poles and the Jews. If it should be asked: By what right? then the answer is, by the right of self-assertion. We Germans want to be leaders in this world because that position is due to us on the basis of achievement." It is the same old story. Dr. Ley knew his audience.

What are the Chances?

12. Can Germany be Democratised?

The democratisation of Germany will not be brought about merely by the demise of Hitler; it can only be brought about by eradication of that deep-seated militaristic and messianic spirit of the German people which made it possible for them ever to welcome Hitler as their leader. His death would probably be followed by an attempt on the part of the High Command to transfer the dictatorship to themselves—indeed, such a transference may even now be taking place— but this dictatorship, no less than Hitler's, can only be overthrown by total unconditional defeat.

Looking to the future, it would be folly to imagine that the process of democratisation of Germany will be either easy or rapid. Democracy, as we understand it in Anglo-Saxon countries, is not so much a political system as an attitude towards community life, which politics is made to serve; but this attitude has taken centuries of experience to evolve. But just as this attitude towards community life has finally become ingrained in us, so, as the result of a very different history, the militaristic Herrenvolk attitude has become ingrained in the Germans.

The Preliminary Surgical Operation

Hitler should be regarded not so much as a cause as an effect, a symptom of a virulent disease with which the Germans have been inoculated for over a century. Granted that Hitler and his accomplices are dealt with with proper severity at the moment of defeat—or, to pursue the simile, that the German nation is subjected to a drastic surgical operation—then in the course of time, with proper guidance and control from outside, the slow experiment of inculcating democracy in Germany may be commenced. But the *sine qua non* is the surgical operation, which must be as thorough and as free of false sentiment as are the surgeon and his knife.

Mercy + Moderation = Weakness

For the German has been brought up to regard mercy or moderation as weakness. Even the sporting instinct which inspires in ourselves clemency towards a beaten foe is invariably misconstrued by the Germans. The armistice of November, 1918, made one cardinal mistake; it imposed *conditions*—which the Germans accepted and then, later, declared they need not have! For to the German, any *conditions*, even severe, suggest a measure of compromise, and compromise implies a measure of weakness. In 1943 we are wiser. Casablanca prescribed "Unconditional Surrender"—a decision profoundly correct both militarily and psychologically. It is the only thing the Germans will understand, because it is what they themselves would impose upon us if they won.

(Several of the quotations are from *Thus Spake Germany*, 1941, edited by W. W. Coole and M. F. Potter. George Routledge and Sons.)

JAPS

British Views on Japan during the Second World War

Army Bureau of Current Affairs

ISBN: 978-1-910375-44-0

www.ingramcontent.com/pod-product-compliance
Lightning Source LLC
Chambersburg PA
CBHW071509040426
42444CB00008B/1567